LIFE IS
NO FAIRY TALE

*Other books by Ursula Bloom
on related themes*

Rude Forefathers
Without Make-up
Mistress of None
The Inspired Needle
Time, Tide, and I
Log of an NO's wife
Parson Extraordinary
The Rose of Norfolk
Price above Rubies
Victorian Vinaigrette
The Elegant Edwardian
Youth at the Gate
Down to the Sea in Ships
War is not Wonderful
Rosemary for Stratford-on-Avon
Rosemary for Frinton
Rosemary for Chelsea
The Mightier Sword
Mrs Bunthorpe's Respects
A Roof and Four Walls
Requesting the Pleasure

URSULA BLOOM

LIFE IS
NO FAIRY TALE

ROBERT HALE · LONDON

© *Ursula Bloom 1976*
First published in Great Britain 1976

ISBN 0 7091 5640 5

Robert Hale & Company
Clerkenwell House
Clerkenwell Green
London EC1R OHT

Filmset by Specialised Offset Services Limited, Liverpool
and printed in Great Britain by
Lowe & Brydone Limited
Thetford, Norfolk

CONTENTS

All the world's a stage,
And all the men and women merely players:
They have their exits and their entrances;
And one man in his time plays many parts,
His acts being seven ages. ...

William Shakespeare

ILLUSTRATIONS

FOREWORD

When one writes of real life one finds it hard,
for it has no mercy. This is a true story – my
own. Much has happened to me – a clergyman's
daughter, brought up in one of the loveliest parts
of England, near Stratford-on-Avon. Personally
I am rather glad that it cannot happen again.

U.B.

1

FROM HEMSWORTH TO WHITCHURCH

I have written many books about my own life, dealing with my personal experiences in a world which has often been unkind to me. But this book is rather different from the others. It is the story that I have not told before. It tells of how in my early days I gained the bitter experience of living life, and I do warn those who read it that it is not amusing, nor is it gay. At times it could be *exceedingly* bitter.

But most certainly this is the way to learn to live one's life; perhaps one has to suffer to understand the problems that living offers.

Most definitely it has taught me how to live so that I could help others in a hard world, and perhaps for this reason I should be grateful for the wide experience of shock and of distressing blows which only hardship can teach so ably.

I was born in a period when the Victorian era was coming slowly to its close, and although we did not know it then, security was disappearing with it. We should never be as strong again. Naturally nobody realized this at the time, for ours was the empire on which the sun never set. God Who made us mighty might make us mightier yet. Or not. That lay in the future.

The Victorians had cultivated the habit of drawing down the blinds on their mistakes, and they always did their best to hide their disappointments from the harsh criticism of the world. The side they showed to life, and the one in their private homes, were not always the same thing. They would only lift the blinds when the drawing-room fires were lit, and all the proper preparations had been made to receive their guests. Mother would be in her best 'receiving' gown, and the ideal tea was prepared, the sort of tea that nobody would have dreamt of having normally.

But drawing down the muslin curtains was not the easiest way in which to live, however successful they may have felt it to be. For muslin *is* transparent! They hoped that the neighbours would never see through their little pretences, the ruses, and the petty hints which gave the impression that they were richer than they were, better born as well, and in an altogether more prosperous position than the neighbours.

My father had been ordained in the parish church at Harlow in Essex, and had gone immediately to his first curacy at Hertford, where he married my mother. Then they went to Harwich, which was a sleepy little town standing in an amiable and contented neighbourhood, where he was happy. His idea was to give his youth and energies to hard work. He was the most hard-working man that I have ever met, and quite untiring. He could wear us all out! But he felt that he had insufficient to do at Harwich, and should be where he was needed more. Purposely he left it, and sought out an entirely different kind of curacy at Hemsworth in Yorkshire. Hemsworth was in the middle of the coal-mining district, and his purpose was to serve others, and give greater help to the men who needed it most. But he *did* find Hemsworth bitterly disappointing.

The miners were extravagant, and he was a man whom poverty had made careful. It worried him, but one could not stop this kind of working man from spending. They 'blew' everything when they got their wages (far more than those in other conditions at that time.) They did not care if they starved for the rest of the week, as long as they had a good weekend. Betting was THE thing!

Everything came out of pawn on pay day, and went back into pawn on Monday! Then, once again, they were 'broke to the wide'. They lived this way.

They bought only the best steak for their racing greyhounds, he told me, and did not care if the children were hungry, as they frequently were. The greyhounds could make money for them, so they said, and one day they believed they would make a fortune this way.

He was shocked by their lack of principle, and worked hard in an attempt to mend their ways, but of course he did not succeed. He told me that living up north had taught him a lot, but that it was not the lesson a man wanted to learn!

When there was a pit disaster (and there were several) he rushed to the minehead in a valiant attempt to comfort the women who waited. He knew that some might already be widows, and he, a deeply compassionate man, wanted to help them. Too often he found they were far more interested to know if the lodger was all right than their own husbands! They were entirely different from the southerner, something that he had never realized before. In the end he came to the conclusion that, try as a man might, he would never change their attitude to life.

But whilst he was living at Hemsworth, he started to put his gift for writing to use. Writing ran in the Bloom family, though none of them had then tried their hands at a novel. My mother inspired him to start with a pen. They were, of course, distressed by the mere pittance on which they lived. The curacy at Harwich had been £120 a year (and a house in West Street). At Hemsworth it rose to £130 a year, and a quite nice house, which I once went to see.

My mother fostered the feeling that, given the chance, my father could write books, and somehow she convinced him sufficiently for him to make a start.

He had been brought up by his grandparents, for his mother had deserted him when he was a month old, leaving him at Castleacre in Norfolk, with his grandparents. He had been born there, in the Old Grove, and there he had been reared.

Educated extremely well by his grandfather, he had started work when he was sixteen years old, teaching in Miss Billing's school for boys. He did remarkably well, for he himself learnt easily, had a miraculous memory for everything, and loved teaching.

Possibly he would have remained a coach all his life, had it not been for Harry Hopkins, one of his grandfather's pupils. Harry was an exceedingly wild young man; ultimately passing into Cambridge, he got very drunk and ran a don round the quad in a wheelbarrow! (That never pays!) My father took his place, and did well there.

It was when living in Hemsworth that he made his first attempt at writing a book. My mother urged him on, and he did better than he had thought.

After three hard years of trying to do good there, and making himself very popular, for he was a lovable man and always kind, *I* changed their plans. I announced that I was on the way!

My father was determined that no child of his should have the word Hemsworth on his or her birth certificate. "We are off to pastures new," he announced. Probably at heart he was a confirmed southerner, and he disliked the north. He sought to return to the part of England that he knew and where he felt at home.

Mr Pearson (father of our famous Arthur Pearson, who founded the magazine world) was the rector of Springfield in Chelmsford, and was advertising for a new curate. My father applied for the job, and he got it. He was good at interviews, a man possessed of the greatest charm, and one who could talk anyone round without a doubt.

He had been blessed with the most glorious good health, and the strength of an ox, whereas Mother was delicate, small (weighing only seven stone), very pale, with hair that greyed in her twenties. She was an extremely good mimic, which at times had got her into a lot of trouble.

At Hemsworth she had engaged a Mrs Jaycock (the wife of a railway guard) to bring me into the world and she would have to come down to Chelmsford. Mrs Jaycock had no nursing qualifications whatsoever, but then nobody thought of having a baby as an illness at all, but rather a perfectly normal thing to do. Even Queen Victoria showed no dismay at employing a completely untrained nurse to look after her.

Down to Springfield went the family, to a little house practically in the prison itself, and it was the most pleasant change for them after the north. My father was thankful that he had done it. They made nice friends, but of course they were never rich. The money given to a curate then was in the vicinity of about £140 a year at the most. Economy was always their first consideration.

Mother went to church one December afternoon (for it was a Sunday) and she came home feeling slightly peculiar. A local woman came in to 'lend a hand', with the result that under five pounds of myself arrived during the evening. Mrs Jaycock came down by train the following morning.

They had wanted a daughter.

What happened next is something that I have never been able to explain, even to myself. My father always said that he lost his head, which I think was a trifle far-fetched. He was doing well at Springfield, immensely popular with the people, and Mother was very friendly with 'the Pearson girls', much her own age. She thought that everything was going admirably, and they were intensely happy about my coming. But was it all so good?

In Springfield, there lived a girl, Annie Archer, then in her late twenties, which almost marked her as being an 'old maid' in those days. It was a good deal older than it is now. She did church work, dusting out, doing the flowers on the third Sunday, and that sort of thing. Also she played the organ for them. I never knew what happened, it was in the organ loft (of all extraordinary places) that my father and she had something in the way of an affair.

The story that went the rounds, was that my father was found there, with Miss Archer, and little more. Mr Pearson took the gravest view of this. Personally I cannot believe that it was anything serious, because I am sure my father would have halted at that, for, as some cynic once said, "he was a man who would paddle, but would never bathe". Born of the Victorian era, he had been brought up by lovesick aunts, all really pretty, and with *beaux* coming and going all the time. He sent valentines, was a first-class 'hand-patter', with the occasional kiss thrown in. It was all very stupid of him, for it is so detectable, the wrong thing for a parson, and could only get him into trouble.

Mr Pearson took it severely and went to the Bishop about this; he also took a grave view of the matter. I lay in my pram knowing nothing of life, when the Bishop stepped in, and for two years my father's job was suspended. It was agonizing for my poor mother. They were terribly hard-up with no stipend now though the Bishop said he would re-consider the matter in two years' time. It seemed to be a very long time.

They left Chelmsford, myself with them.

My father turned to the only other source of income and this was teaching. He had worked for Miss Billing, she had given him a good reference, and now he did have some luck.

There was a boys' school that was advertising for a headmaster, and a house was thrown in. The school was at Long Marston, in Gloucestershire, where it was said that King Charles II turned the spit. My father went to see the authorities and got the appointment. He did well there, for he was an excellent schoolmaster and took a great interest in the pupils.

You would have thought that the worry of all this would have taught my father to be less foolish; it certainly worried Mother, who was horrified, but my father rose like a lark above it all.

They moved in, liked the place, made many friends, and the school prospered. My brother was born in Long Marston in the year 1895. He was extremely delicate and he occupied all my mother's time. I was not a particularly strong little girl, but he was so frail that half his life we had to have a trained nurse with him. It was a vast expense, at a time when my people did not have much spare money, but even though the income was small, they kept a good cook and housemaid, and had a little nurse girl who wheeled me out. In those days everybody kept this sort of staff. Today I look back on it with envy.

Whatever talk there was about my father's behaviour, he *was* a charmer. He got to know the entire neighbourhood, and he made himself intensely popular. He was gaily amusing, and ever-helpful in an emergency, never tiring. At that time the village and its surroundings was a world of well-born people, and he – a good companion – was liked by all of them. He played games well, was a great help at a party, and highly intelligent (except when it came to women, and then he could be – and nearly always was – extremely silly.)

He knew the Roberts-Wests, living at Alscot Park at Preston-on-Stour. Mrs Roberts-West was a great tennis player, very good indeed, and wanted someone with whom to practise. When he could, my father bicycled off to play with her, and they became friends. There was nothing odd about this: she was *not* that sort of woman.

The two years of suspended living was just up when life played a trump card into his hand. He had been born lucky. In the second autumn at Long Marston the bicycle had arrived, so he and Mother went miles this way. It was very much the vogue, and they covered long distances which they had never dreamed of up to then.

They were asked over to dinner at Alscot Park that autumn. It is some considerable way from Long Marston, of course. The old squire, James Roberts-West, was there, his wife with him. Their marriage was not wildly successful, for it was said that the squire had a lady friend living in a mansion in Cowes; most certainly he was very seldom back at home. There were four sons; (Vega, the little girl, had died, a most dreadful blow to them.) Jimmie, the eldest son, had had trouble, for he had married a French actress, and local gossip said that her great reputation had come because she had danced in Paris with only a ring on her big toe! That is possibly some exaggeration, but it was the story they put around. Jack and Reggie, the next two sons, were in the Royal Navy; the youngest one, Algy, was his mother's devoted companion.

Arriving in the park, my parents cycled down the very dark drive, and when they got nearer, Mother got off, unpinning her evening frock, which had been looped up. One could only dine in evening dress in those days, and the frock was a worry on a bicycle. They walked the rest of the way, she holding it up. The front door was opened by Mooring the butler, with an imposing footman on either side of him, strutting along in step. It took three men to open a front door (I cannot think why) and it was most impressive. The footmen did it for the butler would never have touched the handle – it would be 'beneath' him.

The Roberts-Wests got on with us well. After dinner he and the Squire retired to the library to have a talk whilst Mother and Mrs West sat in the magnificent drawing-room that was hung with pale yellow silk, and had remarkable pictures.

It seemed that the living of Whitchurch, where Mr Beale had been resident for some time, was becoming vacant, as Mr Beale was retiring. The Squire offered it to my father. Quite suddenly it looked as if we had drifted into calmer waters. He would be back in a dog-collar, for of course he accepted it.

I must admit that possibly Whitchurch was not everybody's idea of a suitable spot to live in, for it had some bad points. The original village had disappeared in the time of Queen Elizabeth, leaving near the remote church only one cottage which had been originally the rectorial stables. The Church (which contained some windows from Tewkesbury Abbey) was marooned in the fields. It did have the most ghastly approach; how we did it for three times on a Sunday, I shall never know.

The new village had been built by the Roberts-Wests, who had pulled down the old thatched cottages. It was small, comprising only eight cottages and two farms. From it led a gated road which went to Crimscote, known to us as 'the suburb'.

There was also a single farm called Bruton (nearly two miles away) near Admington, but still included in our parish. We were always thankful that those who lived there at the time were Plymouth Brothers, so did not want the parson calling too frequently.

The living was £300 a year, with a fairly large rectory standing in three acres of garden, also stabling and outhouses, but of course, no bathroom. My father when he went to see it (and he was there almost at dawn) believed that he could take pupils and so supplement the stipend.

My mother went with him and she always remembered standing in the massive porch, on that dull December day with snow threatening, and wondering if she was doing the right thing. She looked across the fields to Alderminster, beyond that to Naven Hill, with the odd farm here and there, and she wondered how Fate had dropped this plum into her lap. Then, with anxiety, she asked herself, could the plum be a bitter apple?

She had never forgotten the trouble with Annie Archer at Springfield, and she only hoped that my father had learnt his lesson, but this very week there had been another difficulty. This time it was the little nurse-girl who wheeled out my brother's pram. My father had been kind to her, and apparently the girl had fallen for him. When clearing away the breakfast one morning, Mother had told her to do something she had omitted to do, and the girl turned on her, saying nastily, "I am as much his wife as you are!" This must have been something of a surprise. My poor mother did go through it, I must say. The girl left immediately, of course, and Mother, realizing that my father was scared about the whole thing, herself went to see the parents. By the grace of God, they did not take the girl's part. They said that she was always doing things like that, and they could not think what on earth induced her to do it. Somehow or other – I shall never know quite how – Mother got through that very awkward situation, coming as it did at the very worst time for her.

Of course the Blooms were a flirtatious family, and always had been. But Mother was a very different personality. She had been born at Swaffham, quite close to Castleacre, and all sorts of stories about the Blooms went the rounds there. The Bloom sisters (my father's aunts, all very pretty and, I gather, fairly gay) had started the ball rolling this way. Now, when there was the great chance of my parents' lives, the move to Whitchurch rectory, she was apprehensive, and she paused to think.

She asked herself very seriously, "Am I sure that we are doing the right thing in moving in here?" She was more than a little uncertain.

She had the feeling that at last Fate was offering the second chance, which they needed so much. She prayed that my father would have learnt his lesson. He had suffered for the affair with Annie Archer, which she had never believed was true, saying that Miss Archer had dreamt the whole thing; the little maid at Long Marston had been a hysterical girl, and her parents had told my mother so.

She had got to take this big chance, she had also got to be grateful for it. They moved into the rectory on New Year's Day of the following year.

Whitchurch rectory was built in the rather imposing style of its era – 1840. It was of red brick, with a blue slate roof, and a skylight which lit the landing, and never fitted properly – distressing at times. It leaked in a big storm, and buckets had to be put on the stairs to catch the water. Sometimes we had a regular waterfall coming down those stairs. Some of the windows had been blocked up, and I was always told that this was because of the window tax. There was a drawing-room, a dining-room, and a study for the pupils, where my father would coach them for the university.

When we got in, Mother urged him to do some more writing, for he wrote well. He got in touch with the *Stratford-upon-Avon Herald*, then said to be the best local paper in England, under Mr George Boyden, who was a darling! My father also reviewed the

Festival for a London paper. He was the hardest-worker that I have ever known, and he never tired, going on for ever when he wanted. His were reference books, never novels, because he had no imaginative source at all.

He helped Lady Warwick with *Warwick Castle and its Earls* – In fact he actually did the writing, and she gave him £50 for it. How he fitted in all his literary efforts, with the parish duties, I shall never know, but most certainly, even in his eighties, he was the most energetic man I have ever met!

We were hard-up, of course, but then it was urgent to present a proud appearance to the outside world. We employed a retinue of servants, mainly because it looked good, and was 'the thing'. Later in the new century, just before the First World War, we had only a house-parlourmaid, and cook, and truly they were all that we needed. But, in the late nineteenth century, one had to impress the neighbours with imaginary wealth, and we worked hard to do this.

Our main bother was that we had no carriage. We got about quite well on bicycles, of course, but that is never quite so impressive as riding in a carriage (preferably with a pair of horses to drag it, like the Roberts-Wests.)

The living was just over £300 a year and the pupils paid well, sent to my father for coaching by parents·who could ill afford it. But he *did* get young men through, and it was essential to go to a university in those days. In the end he felt happier with his writing than teaching young gentlemen who did not want to learn how to get to Cambridge.

I was brought up in that tiny village of one hundred and twenty souls, as my father put it. My delicate little brother was always ill, and a tremendous drag on the stipend, poor child! I was more or less an only child.

I was seven years old when the big change came, for my father took over Trinity College in Stratford, whilst the headmaster, Mr Beckwith, was seriously ill. My father was a scholar, and well suited to the job, also an excellent master. He came home to 'take duty' at week-ends, and in cases of need rushed back on the hard-worked bicycle, in this way managing to do two jobs at the same time.

Trinity College was almost entirely intended for the sons of

Service people. Usually the parents were stationed in India, and wished to get the sons into the army as their fathers had done before them. The College had a very good reputation for doing its job well, and not everybody could be temporary headmaster.

The one snag was German lessons, for Mr Beckwith wanted these, and my father was *not* good at languages. Eventually this problem was solved by my mother, who had been educated in Bonn and spoke both German and French fluently. There was some difficulty about a woman giving these lessons in a college for young men approaching their late teens, as some of them were, but, in the end, this was arranged, and three times a week Mother cycled into Stratford to give the German lessons.

At home the house ran on without my father in residence. Those were the halcyon years when, if a maid left, within a few hours one had half a dozen more clamouring round the back door wanting a job.

The family were far too grand even to lift a duster, which would have been *infra dig*.

In the kitchen there reigned a fat woman known as 'Old Cook'. (She was the one who had a private key to Mother's store cupboard, about which Mother did not know a thing, of course). Cook was a knowing old piece. She saw to it that she did nothing else but cook.

There was a house-parlourmaid. She had the 'glass pantry' to herself, where she washed up the silver and the glasses, and if you took a plate to her, you got your nose almost bitten off your face!

There was also a kitchen maid, who worked the hardest of them all, for both of the others made sure that she did.

Then, to add style to the collection, we had a page boy, George Morris (the eldest of the Morris boys) then known as a 'buttons', because of the unending buttons on his funny little jacket! He was the only person in the house to whom my young brother would 'go', for George had six brothers of his own, and he knew all there was to know about babes.

Minnie, our nurse, would take us down to the drawing-room at tea-parties and, when the spirit moved him, my young brother would shriek blue murder, which must have been so nice for the visitors! I know he shocked me considerably, because I had been taught always to behave amiably, and never to shriek, for "only babies did that." He went down in my estimation every time.

The bell would be rung for George to take him back to Minnie. He would come in, see what was required, and then would pick the baby up in the most sturdy manner. My brother would grip hold of George's hair, which I should have thought would have been most painful, but George was extremely courageous, and with all those brothers of his, well-accustomed to the ways that babies behave, and he would bear him away saying in a soothing voice, "There, there," (till he got the other side of the drawing-room doors), when it changed to "Shut up!"

In this household, none of the family ever lifted a finger to do any work. The servants did everything, and if they did not do it very well, out they went. There was no holiday times or half days off. But one must remember that their people came, and had tea with them, and they could go home if they asked whenever possible.

Next door lived the famous Marie Corelli. She was arbitrary, demanding others to do what *she* wished, and a little imperious. At heart, she was a kind, generous woman, spoilt by the fact that she had done so well, and now she was very difficult. And when she got on to that high horse, she did so with tremendous pomposity.

As one mayor once said rather sadly, "Poor Marie Corelli. She forgets that she is not Stratford's only star. We *did* have William Shakespeare before she ever came here."

Of course the trouble was that the lady (whom I always knew as 'Aunt Marie') had done far too well too quickly. She was a very hard worker, I admit, and after an eight o'clock breakfast, would go straight to her desk, never leaving it until eleven. As she finished each page in long-hand, Miss Davis her secretary fetched it for typing! (I would have thought it the most difficult way to work with this goings-and-comings arrangement). At eleven she went out, and her carriage would be waiting outside the front door for her. There would be a big crowd of people to watch, and this happened every day.

She truly believed that she was a genius, and the crowd shared her opinion. She was very arrogant, but good to me, and whatever else one says about her, she *did* give me the first half-sovereign that I had ever had (although I had no idea what it was) when I was seven years old.

She was commanding, and although she did a lot for Stratford she became intensely unpopular. She sent a haughty message to my father at Trinity College, saying that she wished the boys to be quieter during her 'writing hours'. She could not tolerate the noise of the eleven o'clock break. The boys took a dislike to her in no mean manner; and, if there is a community who are good at getting their own back, then it is boys! They took a sheer delight in kicking a football through the windows of her 'winter garden', and they got there many a time. Of course she was furious, which was only natural.

My father, who was in charge, understood how the pupils felt, and he went round in his usual extremely amiable manner, to see the lady about it, and to apologize. He had been born with an amazing power for fascinating women, and especially so when they were past their springtime, and slightly fading! This applied to poor Marie Corelli at this time. My father knew exactly what to say, and he said it rather well. They became friends. He dined with her. That was the night after one of his 'young gentlemen' had been experimenting with some gunpowder. He had been buying it, getting just a little at a time, from a shop belonging to Mr Lacey the ironmonger. He blew up an outhouse in the college grounds, and one of Miss Corelli's trees with it. That would not have been much help, I should have thought.

But they got on magnificently. Interested in his career, she got my father to dine with her and Mr Methuen the next week, and Methuen published his book *Monastic Seals*. Later she got him there to meet Mr Fisher Unwin, who published *Shakespeare's Church* and *Shakespeare's Garden* for him. There was no doubt about it, she was a great help, and she did everything that she could for him. Knowing my father, I am quite sure that he repaid her in the most attractive compliments (he could pour these out) and the occasional pat of the hand, the encouraging smile, and the twinkle in those gaily blue eyes.

She came to the rectory and got on well with everybody, especially with me. She opened the garden fête, and in those days it *was* something to have the famous Marie Corelli on the lawn;

we got crowds from all over the place.

We were going up in the world, and how thankful my mother must have been that we were doing better!

As my father was such a proficient teacher, one would have thought that he would have appreciated the gift of a good education for his daughter, but he completely ignored my own lessons. Education for me was something which I lost by the way! In fact, I never got any.

My mother taught me to read when I was three years old from a wonderful book called *Susy's Six Birthdays*, I have it still. My father insisted that I read widely and could answer questions on the book later. I knew my Dickens, Thackeray, George Eliot, Ainsworth and the poets. I also knew my Shakespeare. Later, I went with him to review the plays during the Festival, which lasted for three weeks in April at the Memorial Theatre, the old one given to the town by the late Mrs Flower. But I never learnt arithmetic. I learnt some French and German from summer-time governesses, but the child in the National schools would have left me far behind when it came to ordinary education.

This caught up with me later. I know when I married (for the second time) a Naval officer, and we were in the south of France, the ship was suddenly about to sail for Malta. My husband thrust some money into my hand, and told me to follow by train via Italy. I had not the faintest idea where Malta WAS! I got a ticket and found it the most thrilling and exciting experience, with four days in the train!

I could never spell at all, and I was crassly ignorant when it came to that sickening performance known as 'doing sums'! I remember that my mother was seriously worried about my lack of education, for she herself had been taught well, and far above the standards of those days, for my grandmother believed in this. After a series of day-schools, where my grandmother always had a row with the headmistress, my mother went off to Bonn-am-Rhein, where she was educated. Apart from reading extensively, my own education was practically nil. To this day I cannot count.

At eleven, I was the only child in a large ladies' orchestra, playing second violin with seven others. I had passed my first, second and third exams. with the Incorporated Society of

Children's Letters.

Aunt Nellie will be very pleased to receive letters from children about their pets, or anything else that may interest them.

Make your communication in form of a letter, written on one side of the paper only. Begin at the top with your address, and the date of the month and year. Sign your real name and age at the end of the letter.

Address to Aunt Nellie, "OUR HOME," 6, Essex Street, Strand, W.C.

Stratford-on-Avon.

Dear Aunt Nellie,—I wish very much to become one of your nieces. I have one dear little brother and no sister. We like drawing and painting. I am six years old, and can play the piano; mother teaches me. I am very fond of dollies; I have six; their names are Winnie, Millie, Mary, Margerie, Oscar, and Evelyn. The two last are boys. My dad is making me a big doll's house; I shall have a large family of dollies live in it. I do hope you will print my letter.

—Your loving niece,

URSULA BLOOM.

Aged 6 years.

How beautifully your letter was written, Ursula! Did you know all the words, or did mother help you with the spelling? Yes, you have got a number of dollies, and very pretty names they have, too.

Brixton, S.W.

Dear Aunt Nellie,—I have never written to you before, although I saw the children's page in OUR HOME, and I am going to tell you about my pets. I have a little canary; his name is Dick, and I had to feed him and put him on a chair for mamma to hang up when she came down, and my pussy came and knocked it over and hurt the bird. I hope to see my letter in print next week.—From your loving little niece.

LILY ADDIE TOFIELD.

Aged 9 years.

I hope Dick is better again; it was rather sad for him to be upset like that. Do you think that pussy did it on purpose? did she want to get at him to eat him?

Perth, Australia.

Dear Aunt Nellie,—May I become one of your nieces? I live in Perth. The soldiers here that were picked for the war are leaving to-morrow. We have a dog called Paddy, he is about nine years old, and a cat named Fluff, and a lot of fowls and chicks and ducks. One of the chickens died to-day, and I was very sorry to lose it, it was such a dear little one. It was three weeks old. I must say "Good-bye."—I remain your affectionate niece,

MAY GREIF.

Aged 8 years.

Did you see the soldiers start for the war, or were you not able to go? How do you like living in Australia?

My first published effort, in *Our Home*, January 1900. I received half a crown for it.

Musicians, years before my time. I was insulted when at ten years old I walked into the examination room and a benign examiner said "Preparatory?" to which I replied "Oh no, Grade One, *not* Preparatory," which I thought was kids' stuff! He was amused. I found no difficulty in music, and this was the career which my parents wanted for me.

My first publication was called *Tiger*, which Marie Corelli had published for me. (Though I had already had a letter printed in the magazine for ladies *Our Home*.) Aunt Marie was always most encouraging about my writing. This was a story of a cat named Tiger. Very unfortunately my parents butted in. They put all the spelling right (it was far more amusing as it had been when it left me), and they added this and that here and there, so that I never felt that it was my own book at all. As it was originally written, it had great personality, one of my strongest points; as it was published, it really stood for nothing.

I wish that Aunt Marie had stayed as a friend, but her great trouble was that she quarrelled with everybody, and in the long run she had no friends left at all. In the end she had a violent quarrel with my father, and so the friendship ceased to be.

I was happy in the village, of course, because I knew no other world. I adored both my parents. I looked after my small brother, although we had little in common, because he, poor child, was always so ill. I would have defended him to the death. I think that I am of one of those people who love others and make friends easily. Possibly I should have enjoyed the crowd of other girls at school, but for me this was not to be. I almost reared myself, and education did not come into it.

The occasional French governess came and 'talked French' to me, or a German who spoke to me in her native tongue, otherwise I was taught absolutely nothing.

Then suddenly, when of course I was far too young to cope with the dreadful complications which followed, life changed. So far I had been dedicated to my parents and my little brother and the complete peace of the glorious Warwickshire countryside which surrounded us. Then everything altered.

It changed too soon for me, and I came face to face with life itself, and I was too young to face it.

2

THE MOVE SOUTH

I must have been about nine and a half years old when I first became vaguely aware of something that was rather 'different' in my world. There is no other word which quite describes it, and it is hard to explain. This difference focussed around my father, of whom I was exceptionally fond, and he really was a most delightful man. But somehow I got a knowledge of something going on, something which was kept secret, and which I did not understand at all.

I rode a bicycle, an old one of Mother's with enormous handlebars, no free wheel of course, and man-size pedals, but it got me places. I was saving every penny I could to buy myself a 'real bicycle' later on, but this was hard going on 2d a week, and occasional birthday money from great-aunts and such. My father and I used to go into Stratford to shop for Mother, to Warwick, and all round, and I became aware of a change in his manner when he talked to a woman whom he liked. He had a special look which came, and it aroused my suspicions.

Obviously I knew nothing of what are called the 'facts of life' and it is extraordinary how ignorant a child can be. They do not fit together the jigsaw-puzzle pieces of love, and for a time remain blind to it. I knew, of course, that mares had colts, and sheep had lambs frequently in the fields about me, and this was going on all the time. But I never associated that sort of thing with human beings. This was farm life, and of course quite different.

It really began with a lot of silly talk from my father. In some ways he had never grown up, and was a mere boy when it came to love affairs, for half of the fun was to talk about them.

I remember his first affair; it was with a woman who lived just outside Stratford and did very good washing and ironing. Mother was an expert embroideress, and the work had to be pressed and prepared when she wanted to show it. She worked most beautifully. Charity (I forget her other name) seemed to me to be quite old, for her hair was grey, and I had to stay outside to "mind the bicycles". Sometimes my father was a very long time, coming out again all bright-eyed and gay, with that funny little smile on his face. Charity would come to the door with him hand-in-hand, and they would have a last few moments on the step, he pressing her hand. I never saw him kiss her, but there was something about his manner which worried me. Instinctively I knew that it was not right, but did not know why.

I told him on the way back that I did not like her, and he said she was sweet and I must learn not to take dislikes to people, for that was *not* the way to get on in this hard world. I never commented on his women friends again.

There were others ...

I do not think there was anything 'wrong'. I believe him to have been a born flirt, who just could not stop flirting though I do not think he tried very hard. Possibly his upbringing in the eighties, with his aunts all keen on getting married, and ceaselessly talking about their love affairs, might have started it. But every little while I would find it happening. That look on his face, and the snigger that came with it, and always for a woman whom I considered to be old. Perhaps I could have understood it if it had been with some pretty girl, but that was not his idea at all.

I was determined that at all costs my mother must never know.

I was devoted to my mother, and I would have done everything for her that I could, and because of this I began what was a protective attitude towards her. I tried everything I knew to shelter her from any knowledge of it. It started when I was about ten years old.

She had made my father write, and now he had really launched himself into the literary world, for Miss Corelli had been a big help to him.

He published an article every week in the *Stratford-upon-Avon Herald* under George Boyden's editorship, and he was a real dear.

I do not say this because whenever I met him he gave me a shilling (immediately saved towards the free-wheel bicycle which I wanted so much) but because he was so good and kind. He published my first little 'piece' in a paper.

My father was kept very busy with his book commitments and his work for the *Stratford-upon-Avon Herald*. All the world and its wife came to Stratford, and he met a large number of famous people, and revelled in it; he was happy, and in many ways prosperous.

The village leant on us. But one cannot confuse this era with the way in which we live today, for life has completely changed in every respect. Now everyone has some means of transport with which to get help quickly in emergency. And there is the telephone. At that time we had no district nurse, and the nearest doctor was five and a half miles away, with no means of getting him except by bicycle. I remember that when I was twelve years old, a man came to the rectory for help at two in the morning, saying that his father was dying. My own father was away, my mother was ill, so on the spur of the moment – believing it to be my duty – I got out my bicycle and rode into Stratford to fetch the doctor for him. I recollect how furious the doctor was at being called up, and said he did not think he could do any good; why should he come? I was very forward and rude to him, for I said, "If I can come all this way in the dark to fetch you, the least thing you can do is to come back to the poor man." I was very angry.

And he did come!

I can remember standing there and saying it, very much ashamed of what I thought was rudeness to an adult (unheard of in that era) as the dawn was just coming through behind the Guild Chapel. You do not forget that sort of experience in a hurry.

My parents were angry with me for going, then a little proud, and when I told my father how rude the doctor had been, he comforted me. I remember him saying "I should not mind. He's a chapel man, anyway, so you could hardly expect much else from him, could you?"

I was, of course, enchanted that we were not going to live in

Worcester, which I felt I should not have liked. I should have hated to leave the little village, of which I am still really very fond today, but in the end I had to leave it — certainly *not* for preferment!

It was when I was eleven years old that I had discovered that my father was a born flirt. In some ways he was so brilliant, and so sophisticated, but in others he was quite irresponsible. I do hope this is not an unfair conclusion at which to arrive, but he did prove this to me, quite disastrously, later on.

Perhaps I changed a little because of these flirtatious ways of his. He always took me visiting with him, possibly to play gooseberry, so this had become apparent to me. I never knew the exact moment at which this knowledge made itself felt. I was aware that something was very wrong, even if I had been taught that parents could do no wrong. I think the first disillusion came with Mrs Canning.

I met her the first time, cycling back from Warwick with my father, and we dropped into a little tea-house recently opened by the roadside, on the way to Stratford. It was called Coplow. This was run by a Mrs Canning, a charming woman, not pretty, but extremely amusing. She and her husband had split, leaving her with two little daughters, 'Bimbo' and Phyllis, both much younger than I was.

Apparently my father knew the place well, and of course he never missed the chance of seeing her. She was the daughter of a farmer, and had several sisters, most of whom were friends of my father, for he was extremely versatile.

We propped our bicycles up outside, and went and got some tea. Soon after, it was suggested that I should have "a nice look at the garden" and could pick myself a few flowers for my bedroom. This was the same old ruse that I knew by heart! Mrs Canning painted in pastels, and quite beautifully. I think the affair began with his genuine desire for helping her and he *did* help her, for he got her several portrait commissions. She painted both himself and Mother, myself three times, and she exhibited in a big way.

She came to stay at the rectory, and she would spend the week with us, doing this. Mother liked her, for she was gaily amusing, and they got on extremely well together. But very soon I knew that 'something funny' was going on, something which I did not entirely understand. I would come across my father in some far corner of the very large garden, kissing her, and I knew that this was not the right thing to do. Grown-up people, who were not married to each other, did not kiss each other, only children did this. It worried me, but I squashed it on the argument that it was wrong to criticize my father, and that this was my ignorance of life, for undoubtedly one's parents could do no wrong! Let me explain that I *was* very young, and the rectorial life is extremely earnest about these matters, and does not discuss them.

But of course instinct tried to guide me, and sometimes instinct is an alarming teacher. Mrs Canning's sister 'Lit' (so called because she was so small, and my father adored very small women), came to stay with us. I found him kissing Lit in the orchard, and this made me even more worried.

One thing was quite plain, and after a while, I came to realize this. He never did this in front of anybody which gave me the impression that it was a secret. I protected my little brother from any knowledge of it, and blinded myself to it, on the principle of "Honour thy father and thy mother". Maybe I was the one doing wrong in criticizing him.

My father had been engaged to several different girls before he eventually married my mother. I got worried, for there was something deep down inside me which warned me that this was all wrong, and it was not so easy to dismiss this warning. My father, ever an early riser, kindly took Mrs Canning her morning tea in bed and stayed some while with her, with the door locked behind him. Mother was always a heavy sleeper, as I knew, and she had no idea.

I was both young and earnest, made worse by the fact that a remote cousin of mine whose parents were in India, spent the summer holidays with us, and he eloquently tried to inform me of the facts of life. He knew everything. I did not believe a word he said, but then the goings-on in the home did make me slightly unsure. The child senses danger very differently from the way in which the adult does. Adoring my mother, I felt that whatever happened it must be kept from her, even at the cost of telling a lie. The protective instinct for others has always been something that was very strong within me, sometimes to my detriment.

I know now that it would probably have been far better if I had gone straight to my mother and told her the truth, and so got myself rid of the whole thing, leaving her to cope with it, which I could not.

But again there came that dreadful apprehension that one did not 'tell'. Telling on someone was extremely wrong, and no nice person ever did it.

This went on for two years, for my father was one of those men who never seem to lose an old love. He clung on to his childhood's sweethearts in an extraordinary manner of his own, and they pestered and pursued him, but he never got rid of them.

During part of the time I was very happy, because we had a lovely life at Whitchurch, with a house and garden which I loved with all my heart, lots to do, and plenty of time in which to do it. I was sorry that my parents had quarrelled with Aunt Marie at Mason Croft, but this had happened, as it sooner or later always did with Marie Corelli. I doubt if the poor woman ever kept a friend for long, because invariably she flared up in the long run and in this manner made herself very unpopular.

These conditions must have gone on for several years, and then suddenly my mother found out, and it all came to an end. I had nothing whatever to do with it. I had kept it entirely from my mother, guided by an intuitive feeling, not based on any instruction or knowledge. I liked both Mrs Canning and her sister, but they worried me, for I knew that something which I did not understand was going on. Then Fate took a hand, as my friends tell me it always does.

I was fourteen at the time when my father got the job of translating and cataloguing the deeds in Worcester Cathedral – just his cup of tea. He would go there for three or four days in mid-week, staying with Canon Wilson, and returning to Whitchurch for week-end services. The Wilsons asked me there the week before Whitsun, and I adored Worcester. Their lovely house overlooked the Severn and the view of the Malvern Heights. They had a private door into the cloisters, and the

Edgar Tower were the library was, and I ran to and fro and knocked my ankle several times on the stone steps.

Bicycling home from Stratford at the week-end, it was hurting quite a lot, and I went lame. During the Whit Sunday week-end it got considerably worse, and although I started I could not get down to the church to help with the decorations, which worried me, for I hated slacking. I got as far as Mr James's farm, which would be about half way, and had to admit that I could not do it, and limped home, trying not to cry. It hurt me really terribly, and no wonder.

Two ex-pupils who had known my father when at Trinity College, visited us, and one of them was considerably worried about me, for he thought he knew what it was. He had had something like it as a boy, and it was necrosis. He thought I ought to see a doctor at once. That night Mr Earnshaw Hewer F.R.C.S. came to me and verified this.

He thought that I was starting a necrosis of the fibula; it was either that or rheumatic fever, but he thought it was the former. None of this conveyed anything to me. If it was necrosis, it would have come from a blow. Had I hit my ankle badly when riding my bike (I constantly fell off it)? Florence came forward. Florence Huckfield (now our parlour-maid) had kept an eye on us after nannies had ceased to be, and she was a dear. We always went to Florence when in any trouble, and she said I had *not* hit my ankle.

Then they attributed it to the stone steps in the Edgar Tower at Worcester. They might have to operate. They did this on the following Monday, when I was screaming with the pain.

This operation was performed in what we should now call very primitive conditions. The kitchen table, scrubbed hard, was got up the back stairs (I shall never know how) and put up at the end of the bed. I had been taken into Mother's bedroom at the front of the house, away from my own, which looked west on to the black and white forge on the old village green, and Jacques' farm. I was not frightened, for I trusted Mr Hewer completely, and knew that he would look after me; also there had arrived a sweet little Scottish nurse from Fraserburgh, which was a long way to come to the heart of England.

They all promised me that I should be better and almost out of pain when I came to, but when this happened, it was to hear myself shrieking. The pain was even worse.

That was the start of the worst summer of my life! I had one operation after another, and that wretched kitchen table was standing at the end of the bed (ready for them to amputate the foot) for days. Nobody expected me to keep my foot. The thought of that did not worry me so much (for I would have done everything to get out of the sheer agony.) Mother and the nurse never seemed to leave me, and at the worst point, Mr Hewer stayed with me for two whole nights.

It was he who found out something more than he had expected! In my delirium, it came out how worried I had been about my father's love affairs, where I so frequently had had to play gooseberry! Instinct had warned me that none of this was right, in the way that instinct does this work. I had worried about it, for I have always been a very conscientious person, and I talked. Already Mother had heard sufficient, though Mr Hewer did not know this. She had had previous experiences with my father; possibly deep down in her heart the doubt had ever been there, and what a terribly disturbing doubt it must have been for her!

I had now come to the age when I knew that clerical gentlemen could get themselves unfrocked, because from nine years old I had been an ardent reader of the newspaper. Also, unbeknownst to the family, I shared on Sundays the *News of the World* with the cook. There was an odd boy who came round on Sundays (much to my father's disgust, of course), and she got this. Dad never knew that I adored it.

Mr Hewer found that there was more behind all this with my father than he liked, and he suggested that for ten days I should see only the nurses, and my mother. He would rather I was left entirely to women.

I have no idea what I let out in those drifts of unconsciousness! I could hear someone screaming in the distance, and did not know that it was myself, but when I got a little better, I realized a change in Mother. I had aroused all her suspicions, and I was the last person who would have wanted to do this.

My father, James Bloom, in 1940

My mother, Polly Bloom, in 1913

Perhaps she had believed that he would turn over a new leaf in life, and, because he had got back into the church, would value it, and behave properly. She was wrong. Poor thing, she suffered dreadfully during that illness of mine, but would never let anybody see her cry. She used to wander off into the kitchen garden, she told me, and have a good cry by the cucumber frame, and get over it that way!

I had even given away the names of Mrs Canning and her sister, so that Mother knew who was more closely associated with him at this time. Personally, looking back on this, I do not believe that there was more than silly flirtation in it, I remember a man friend discussing the matter with another friend, and not realizing that I could overhear. He said "Bloom can't keep off the women, and he is such a bad chooser."

Perhaps that was so. But even if it was, it could hardly convince an irate Bishop, as Mother knew, and he *had* been in trouble previously and been suspended because of it. I think we both knew that we were on what is called a 'sticky wicket'.

My father spent most of his time at Worcester doing the deeds there, which had been a big financial help, though he had never earned as much as he deserved, for he was most diligent and conscientious at his work, and a brilliant scholar. I am sure that Mother never thought that there was anything more in it, for she believed that having got back into the church, he would have the good sense to behave well. But I think he felt fairly safe, and when he thought this was so, he waived his scruples.

He did not always stay with Canon Wilson, but the cataloguing of the library took him the best part of two years. Later he contrived to stay in rooms, just outside the cathedral close. A nice woman, who told marvellous fortunes with cards, kept the rooms, and she had a daughter called Violet. I knew that my father and Violet got along very well together, and I was extremely anxious about it all, because I saw him kissing her, and that always worried me.

At this time of my life I did not know what to do. I felt that my father was playing with fire, and I did not know how to stop it. It was difficult to associate the seventh commandment with him, but I had a vague idea that this was what it had come to. I think the truth was that he had never outgrown his schoolboy days, and he *would* talk about his peccadilloes. He liked to be considered something of a 'naughty boy' at a time when promiscuity was not the mode, and this even if at Warwick Castle there was always a stir, with the Stratford police clearing the road for the King of England to get down quickly in his car, whilst Lord Warwick slipped out the back way and went off somewhere else!

But what Lady Warwick could do, was not what my father could copy; he seemed to have forgotten that he was a priest, and one who had a black mark already set against him.

Towards the end of my long drawn-out illness, Mother found out, I never knew how. Of course he said that there was nothing in it, and there he may have been quite right, but there was quite sufficient in it to get him out of his dog collar again if the powers-that-be found out, and this, the second time, there would be no further chances. Out he would go, and out he would stay.

Fortunately he and the Bishop were very good friends, and I have always thought that my clever father relied on the friendship too much.

Just before my collapse with necrosis, he had helped the Bishop very considerably, when Lord Portman and his wife came to live at Goldicote House. The Portmans had bought this place, just outside Ettington, in the parish of Alderminster, where Mr Thrupp was vicar. Mr Thrupp was a loyal churchman, very high church, and he did *not* admit divorce. Claud Portman's first wife had divorced him, and Mrs Portman had divorced her first husband. In Mr Thrupp's eyes they were not married. Both had sworn "till death us do part", and death had *not* parted them. He refused them Communion.

Nobody could have shaken Mr Thrupp's loyalty, we all knew, and of course he was right. The Bishop tried pressure, and failed. The Portmans were breathing blood and fire, and in the position to make an awful lot of trouble. But nothing in this world would have made Mr Thrupp give in on one of the ten commandments; you could throw him out, or do what you wished, but he would *not* give them Communion, because, in his eyes, they were not married.

Claud Portman (one can imagine he was seething) swore that he would go to the Press, and he had tremendous influence. The Bishop was now really worried, for the London newspapers were on his tracks already and making the most of it. Out came my father's bicycle, and he pedalled off as some consoling angel. He did not return to tea, or supper, but was doing fine! He suggested they came to *his* church, only three miles further off, and the whole of the horrifying problem was solved.

I do not think that my father appreciated at the time quite what he was letting himself in for. The Portmans arrived next Sunday in our tiny little church in the fields, Mr and Mrs leading the procession in a carriage and pair, a second carriage and pair with a governess, nannie and three children; then two shooting-brakes, the first with female servants, the second with footmen and so on. The village came out to watch. Where *could* we seat them all?

But how well the collection did!

In my illness, the Portmans were goodness itself to me, even supplying a wheel-chair when I got to that stage, and I do owe them an enormous debt for all they did_ I only hope that my father's action helped to repay some of their kindness.

I recovered slowly, and when I took up my ordinary life again, I could not believe how things had changed. Now Mother knew the truth that I had kept from her for so long. Mr Hewer also knew it, for I had raved "Don't kiss her, Daddy! Mummy would not like it," but being a doctor he would not take sides with it. One thing he insisted, which was that at no cost must I be worried over it. I had been dangerously ill. How I ever lived through it, I shall never know, and am sure that I could not have done so had it not been for Mr Hewer's brilliance, and the way that he sat up with me and would not leave me.

Now he wanted me to have peace. I was a long way from that.

Marie Corelli had, I am sure, started my father on the right course, and after the quarrel came (something that seems to have been inevitable with this poor lady) he was commissioned to help Lady Warwick with the book that she was writing called *Warwick Castle and its Earls*. He did all the research work for it, spending mid-weeks at Warwick Castle, and working there.

Lady Warwick (the beautiful 'Daisy') was extremely kind to him, and said to be the most beautiful woman in England. I know the first time that I saw her I thought her to be this, and was carried away by her.

I did go with my father occasionally, for Maynard Greville, her third son, was about my age, and we played together. Lord Brook and Lady Marjorie Greville were much older – I thought of them as being grown-up. There had been a second son, who had died as a baby and was said to be King Edward VII's child, then Maynard, whose father seems to have been unknown. There were many wild guesses, but Lord Warwick's name never came into it.

It was at Warwick that my father moved forward a great deal. I loved it, of course, when I went over, and adored Lady Warwick, who was a real charmer.

Maynard and I used to work the portcullis when we could get up into the room (we couldn't very often, for frankly we were no good at it) and one day we let it down on a visiting Bishop who was *not* pleased!

Now with Methuen and Fisher Unwin buying from him, and the success of *Warwick Castle and its Earls*, my father was doing quite well. But success had turned him back to his old flirtatious self, the one which had already led him into such a great deal of trouble.

I was eleven when my father was offered preferment, a living in Worcester itself, and he refused it. He was a countryman at heart, and he did not wish to move into a city. I know now that he should have taken the chance when it was offered to him, but we all loved our dear little Whitchurch, and worked hard to do what we could for it. I was sure that my father felt that if he left, he would in a sense be failing the people, and he could have been right. They worshipped him, knowing that there was nothing that he would not do for them. Also the country gave him time for his writing and he could review the plays at Stratford; so we stayed on.

We did the wrong thing, but did not know it.

I was growing older, and had come to the stage when I found his flirtations getting a bit too much.

I was afraid for the future.

I had ever since I could remember been a sort of chaperone to him, going to visit some women he had found and "rather liked", and being dismissed to pick a few flowers – anything to get me out of the way. Sharpening with adolescence, I woke up to the fact that none of this could lead to anything that was helpful. I knew that my mother would strongly disapprove, and gathered that she was beginning to find out more. My father dismissed my fears with "Oh well, your mother never understood that sort of thing. It's nothing."

I was at the age when I was devoted to both parents, and trusted them both. It worried me to death when my father spoke like this, because all the time I was convinced that what he said was not right. He liked flirting, and said that all men did. I was at a loss. I did not know what to do or what to say, and he was a man who loved a confidante, and this was what I had become to him.

The personal relationship between my mother and myself was extremely close, and I became more and more protective. I wanted to help her. I always had the foreboding that something would happen and upset everything.

That summer my father became ill. He had overworked, of course, one of the habits of the Blooms. He had been cataloguing and translating the deeds at Rochester at the time, and he began a bad series of abscesses, one after the other, nine in all. When he recovered, Mr Hewer said that, expensive or not, he must have a holiday. There was a general round-up of the finances. Even my own money-box had to go, I think I contributed about eight and twopence at the time, and was most worried. I have always been an inveterate saver of money, and throughout the year saved meagre halfpennies to get together sufficient to pay for a 'fly' to take my brother and myself to a children's party when Christmas came. This year with summer already here to be eight and twopence down looked very bad indeed for me.

My father wrote glowingly from Lynmouth and Weston-super-Mare where he had found cheap boarding-houses, and was, so we gathered, already feeling considerably better for it. He returned to us, his old gay self, but I thought he was a bit too gay. He was one of those men who got a tremendous 'kick' about telling his story to somebody else. Half the joy of having fun lay in the telling, and I was the wretched recipient of his confession.

He had found such very nice people in the boarding-house where he had stayed, especially one charming lady who was there with a girl friend. They were about forty, I understood, which was sheer old age to me.

Probably because now I was growing older and more observant, I noticed even more about my father. He had got on extremely well with Miss Josephine Sims and her friend. She was, he told me, the sister of the Mayor of Bath, with whom she lived. I gathered that she was charming, they had had some lovely trips together, and my father returned home in love.

This was, of course, no new story for my father, who always enjoyed a bit of a thrill *sub rosa*, and Miss Sims had taken the whole affair very seriously. She had gone back to the Mayor of Bath (who was a local draper) and had told him that she had fallen in love with the most charming clergyman, and had given her brother details of her romantic affair with my father.

I might have been very young, but this was no new story for me, and I smelt trouble. It seemed that my father would never learn. The Mayor of Bath was furiously angry and he had said that whatever happened she must give up my father, or leave the house for ever. He was not allowing his silly sister to carry on with a middle-aged married clergyman.

To my father it was an excitingly romantic situation; to me it looked like being a disaster. I begged him to abandon the whole idea, but of course he was not that sort. He adored a romance, and here it was. But never before had he been up against an indignant mayor who refused to tolerate the situation! He gave his wretched sister six weeks in which to make up her mind, which I thought was very fair, and then he turned her out. She wrote suggesting that she came to live with us, and could earn her living by "doing-the-flowers-or-something".

I did not know what to do about it, whatever happened Mother must not know a word. I suppose that I was growing up. At fifteen one feels a woman, and this year the two boys who came as P.G.O's to the farm, came again, and Geoffrey (the younger of the two) suggested that when we both grew up we should get married. I do hope I was nice about it. I was a bit 'off' marriage, thought it was rather a 'poor show', and said so. Geoffrey was killed in the First World War, and I only hope that I was not too terse with him then.

But the affair with Josephine Sims was not cooling down. My father confided in me, and I begged him to be reasonable. There was so little that I could hope to do, and he kept seeing her on his trips away from the rectory, and this only warmed the whole thing up even more.

My horror still was that Mother would find out. What could I do then? She would hate the whole situation, and my father had got the idea of getting Josephine into the house. In the end he suggested this to Mother. He thought Miss Sims would make herself useful. She could act as a general help in the home as she had done for her brother. Mother's response was definitely formidable. She would NOT have it!

I had always thought that one day Mother would find out about this sort of thing, and now it had come. I was, of course, entirely on her side, but aghast at the prospect of what lay ahead of us. I broke down.

When you are only fifteen years of age, your father's childish love affairs become something of a burden to bear, and I had been trying to keep quiet about them for years. Mother now discovered that Mrs Canning, who had painted such lovely pastel portraits, had been what she called "another one of them". She wrote her a quietly dignified letter, asking her not to come to the rectory again, after which there was a complete silence. It was then that my father left on his desk a letter from an old love of his, Adelaide Marsh, and apparently they had been corresponding for some time. There was another violent row.

To a girl recovering from a most painful and dangerous illness, this sort of thing was terribly difficult to bear. I had never thought that our deep happiness in the home could be so entirely wrecked. I was a child who loved my parents, and now I made myself thoroughly ill about it. We were still threatened with Miss Sims as an unpaying guest, because she had nowhere else to go, and more letters kept arriving from Adelaide Marsh.

My father never knew when to stop!

The affair with that wretched Miss Marsh had begun again when she sent him some ridiculous Valentine, and he was flattered by it.

Life in the rectory, which I adored, was rapidly becoming most difficult. My father needed help, but would never do what was asked of him, and we came to that ghastly condition known as 'keeping it from the servants'. Whatever happened, *they* must have no clue as to what was going on! though I am sure that they knew a great deal more than any of us imagined.

That was one of the most ghastly summers. My father and mother would have a row after I had gone to bed, in the brave attempt to "keep it from Ursula". Then she would rush out of doors, and when he could not find her, he would come for me to help him. I was so afraid that she would go down to the river, and attempt to drown herself there, because she was utterly distracted. She could easily have done it, for the Stour was a most dangerous little river with unexpected deep holes in it, which the villagers called "them whirly-pools".

I would, in the end, find my mother, and bring her home, and into my own bedroom to sleep, so that they did not have further rows, but it was hard going. I had to get her across the landing to her own room before the servants arrived at half past seven, bringing up the hot water, lest they smelt a rat.

In the end it was Mr Hewer, the kindly doctor, who stepped into the breach. I got the most horrible attack of measles, and even went unconscious with it. Whether I said something silly (I rather think I did) I do not know, but he found out that I was worried to death about the strange affair going on in the rectory between my father and my mother.

The autumn was coming. He made the suggestion that for the first part of the winter we took rooms in Stratford. I think he was worried for me. He said my father would find how very uncomfortable he was without us, and it would be far better for me. A winter alone in the rectory might teach him the lesson that he ought to learn. I felt wretched. I was too young to be critical, anyway, and too worried about everything.

The continual rows had got me down in a big way. Joscelyn was at boarding school at Wolverley, so it did not bother him. Thank Heaven: he knew very little about it, and this was to the good. A widowed parishioner, dear old Mrs Marshall, moved into the rectory, and with her a maid.

It is all wrong to love a home so devotedly I have found in my life, but I was dedicated to that home and it meant everything to me. My father would allow us £120 a year, saying that Mother had "means of her own", just under £40 all told, left to her by my grandmother.

I shall never forget the horror of that drive away and up the lane, looking back at the village through the dimness of a November afternoon with the fog rising over the river, and the rectory on the side of the hill. I knew then that part of me, a very real part, would live on there for ever.

But we ourselves were going away.

* * *

When we got to the boarding-house in Stratford I found it thrilling in its own way. I had never thought of living in a town, with the lighted streets at night, so different from home, where we had had always to use lanterns.

I had been brought up in an entirely secluded life, for there were no people of our own type in the village, and the farmers and the workers were always intensely busy. The demands of the crops and of the animals were always with them, I had of course known no other life.

But coming into the town was something new to me. I could not understand the sound of footsteps on the pavements at night when the curtains were drawn and the darkness had come. I had lived in a world where there was so seldom any sound at all. There were shops to look at, people to know, things to do that I had never done before, and it was something of a real thrill to me. It seemed to me as though life gave us a brief spell of comfort, though all the time I had the vague sense of apprehension within me, but then I had grown so used to being apprehensive that I could not lose it.

There was of course a certain anxiety about how the Bishop would take our coming to stay in Stratford for a time. We had told everybody that it would be only for a couple of months or so, for the rectory was damp and the river mist got into the house. The doctor wanted me to be somewhere that was warmer, and this all fitted in with the bad illness I had had with my foot.

I longed for the gracious home and the lovely garden, though at this time of year the house was cold and draughty, for the big skylight was none too watertight, and there had been times when we had had to fit up the stairs with buckets because of the leakages.

The little boarding-house was at the corner of John Street, and opposite to Dr Thompson's house; it was friendly and quite comfortable, but Mother fretted very much. She kept saying that time would pass and things would get better, but I was not so sure. I wanted everything to change back again, but of course life does not work that way. A crisis approached us.

We had been there only a few weeks, with Christmas round the next corner, when suddenly at dusk one evening my father burst in on us. He had come for help, because there was trouble, and it was the sort of trouble in which he seemed to specialize.

The one thing about it which helped was that whenever he was in a jam, one could rely on my father to tell the whole story.

At Whitchurch there was of course no Sunday post. The letters got as far as Preston or Alderminster, the two villages on either side of us, and stayed there. If you wanted the letters, you could bicycle over and get them from the cottage which was marked POST OFFICE, and the old lady would give them to you. If not, you waited until the Monday morning and the postman delivered them round about eight o'clock, when we had breakfast.

As usual my father was writing to some woman or other, and felt her letters to be urgent, so he fetched them. I think he had never entirely grown up in his ways, and was still a schoolboy at heart – he acted like it anyway.

In the winter we had an afternoon service, for if you crossed the meadow in the dark you fell over sleeping cattle and that sort of thing. When afternoon service was over, apparently he went

off on his bike to fetch the letters, and this had been going on for
some time. Being a most amiable and friendly man, he would
stop to talk to people whom he met, and this quite simple habit
of his had got him into serious trouble.

There was a family, two sisters and a brother, living in the
village, and the brother came to our church, so when he saw him
my father stopped and spoke to the sisters as well. Somebody had
noticed this, and had sent an anonymous letter to the Bishop
saying that we had left the rectory because of it. They insisted
that my father was always visiting these girls "after dark", for
this was when he fetched those wretched letters, and now one of
them was pregnant.

It was all quite untrue, of course, and there had been nothing
like that, as the girl was *not* pregnant this was just village gossip
that gets around. They say it about every girl at some time or
another, with the smallest provocation.

The trouble was that my father had not got the reputation to
stand up to this sort of thing, for this was far from being the first
time that he had been connected in a scandal. Neither of us
thought for a single moment that there was anything behind it.
The worry was that the Bishop must have known a great deal
about him. What did one do next? It was my mother who took
control.

She was a very clever woman and she was the woman who
could act, I have always felt that she was also quite the bravest
woman I have ever known. She did not reproach him, but she
admitted that at this moment our fate was hanging in the balance.
Undoubtedly he could afford no more scandals. If this new
scandal went any further, it would be a catastrophe.

The next day was a Friday, which is market-day in Stratford-
on-Avon. The little stalls went up in Bridge Street and the yards
of the Unicorn were crowded with farm carts. Everyone comes
into the town to do their shopping, or to sell their wares. The
talk about my father would be something they would chat about.

Mother got in touch with the girl that morning; she was
sympathetic and sorry for her, not reproachful at all. The facts
were wrong, for she was not pregnant, and most indignant. So was
my mother, who was on her side.

I was quite terrified.

I knew only too well, however bravely my father talked about "living things down", that he had a past history which at any moment might crop up. In addition the Bishop was extremely worried about it. If it came to a real row, would he have a leg left to stand on? And if he was prevented from earning, where should we go, and what should we do?

Mother faced up to it with tremendous courage and on the afternoon of market-day, when everything was at its height, the three of us walked out into the streets, my parents arm-in-arm! I saw people turning to look at us, then whispering together, and nudging one another. Mother faced it with complete calm, even though she heard people saying, "Look! That's him! You know what they say ..." and all that sort of thing.

When we came to personal friends, we stopped and spoke to them. We were a perfectly happy and contented little family, doing a spot of shopping. To those who saw us, it was quite plain that there was no quarrel. We were happy together.

On the Sunday, both Mother and myself cycled over to Whitchurch, and I played the harmonium for matins, Mother for the afternoon service. There was no question of my parents having split for good, as everybody was apparently saying. The story we told was perfectly true. The doctor wanted me to spend the winter in Stratford because it was warmer than Whitchurch.

The outward and visible signs of our contentment with one another, were something which made it far more difficult for people to throw mud at us.

My father in a highly penitent mood would do anything that he was told, relying entirely on Mother to get him out of it. He was apologetic too. He even bought me some chocolates, for I had had a collapse when we got home. It had been a little too much, for I had heard some of the rude remarks going on about me and they had shocked me very much. I did not get over it for quite a long time.

The Bishop never took action.

Mercifully he was one of those men who dislike anonymous letters, and also he was a personal friend of my father.

The one who got out of all this the best was my brother who

was at boarding-school near Kidderminster (paid for by his rich godmother, who had been at school with my mother in Bonn). By Christmas when he came home for the holidays, things were better. But Mr Hewer was not too happy about me. Something was wrong with the glands in my throat, I had fits of crying, and the truth was that I had been through too much.

We stayed on in these nice rooms until the spring was advanced. Then, with the Shakespeare Festival coming on, we were told that the cost of them would go up, and we had to move because we could not face the expense. We went into rooms in the Shottery Road, which were much more reasonable because they were almost out of Stratford itself. But I wanted a home, and I found a small house in a row along the Shottery Road, number 41. We managed to rent it at 10s. a week. It was not very pleasant, with a front room, and a back one, a box staircase and two very small and two bigger rooms above it. The kitchen was outside in the yard, an outside shed really, with a cooker and a copper in it.

There was a narrow garden, flanked on either side by the strip of land similar in every house. There were rows of potatoes and rotting cabbages, but never a flower, and Whitchurch had had extensive beds of flowers. On Mondays out came the washing everywhere long lines of it.

On one side of us a very nice policeman lived on the other the young man who was the gondolier for Miss Corelli's gondola, and his wife. (Miss Corelli had got a gondola to advertise herself with – it was the only such vessel on the Avon.)

If we asked anybody in for a little music in the evenings, which we were accustomed to doing, neighbours banged on the door, or yelled rude remarks through the letter box. We had taken it on a three-year lease, and the landlord was a most dreadful little man who, having taken us in, then wanted to get us out. We were, of course, the wrong type of person for a workman's road, and everything we did was (to them) wrong, just as what they did seemed to us to be unpleasant. I must say that we went through a very bad time there at first, though the policeman was kindness itself, and would have done anything to help us, and did. A woman came in and did the work of the house for sixpence a morning, and she was a darling, but it was not a good idea, and could never really work out.

It was then that I started on the river life. I rowed daily, and would punt up to Hatton Rock and back, which is no mean trip. At the new bathing pool, I did a lot of life-saving. My injured ankle had stopped me going in for games, so that it was a real delight to find what a joy the river could be to me. The summer was quite lovely.

But when the autumn came again, it struck me that Mother was none too well. I thought she looked what I would have called "rather grey", and I worried for her. In the end I did persuade her to see Mr Hewer about this. I had the most implicit faith in him, and no wonder, for he *had* saved my foot.

He was none too pleased about it, for he admitted that he had found something that he did not like. Ever since my sister had been born in the first year of her marriage, Mother had had a small lump in her breast. We understood that a gland had gone wrong, and had hardened, and that it was 'nothing'. Mr Hewer did *not* like it, and said that she would be far better off without it. Nobody ought to keep anything of that kind, it could do no good. She had to admit that perhaps it was a shade bigger than it had originally been, and he decided to remove it.

It was extremely worrying, for she would have to go to a nursing-home recently started in the Evesham Road. Her old school-friend, my brother's godmother, who had always been so helpful, made this possible. It was run by two nurses who were dears and quite young, but unfortunately it was on the road to the cemetery, so that when you were well enough to sit up at the window, you saw all the funerals passing by. My brother said that "you could see what you had missed", but not everybody would take it that way.

I was desperately anxious for her.

My father gave us some more money, all that he could spare at the time, but anything was welcome. I realized that the lump would have to be analysed, and it could be dangerous, but I just prayed that it would be all right. My personal feeling was that we had been through such hard times that surely God could not keep on trying us?

After the operation she felt miserable, and the lump went to Birmingham for analysis. She was a very brave woman who never made a fuss, and I was furious that my father hardly went to see her. He and I had a crashing row in that wretched back yard of ours. He was being difficult.

A week later Mr Hewer dropped a note in our door, asking me if I would go along and see him that afternoon.

I went along. I knew that by now he would have received the analysis from Birmingham. He lived in Church House, the big handsome house at the top of Church Street, where Dr Nason had lived before him, looking down the pleasant street to the Guild Chapel. It was known in the town as 'the doctor's house'.

I went into his consulting-room, and we sat down on either side of the fire. On the mantelpiece was the pickle bottle with my rotten old fibula in it, and another with Eddie Portman's appendix. Mr Hewer always said that these two were his mascots, and all I can say is, thank God if my unhappy ankle had done somebody some good. It certainly did nothing for me!

I got the impression that he was worried. He said he had sent the specimen to Birmingham for analysis, and now had got their report, which he handed across to me. It was difficult for me to understand, for they used Latin, and my knowledge of this language was limited, but the whole thing boiled down to the one dreaded word (the one which I had feared all along) – carcinoma.

When I read it in plain typewriting everything seemed to go stone cold within me. Instinctively I knew that I had read a death warrant, for that was what it was. I paused, trying to pull myself together. It would not be yet. It was not now, but ahead of us there it stood, with the shrouded window, the drawn shutters, and her voice quietened for ever.

I did not think that I could bear it.

At that moment, one which unfortunately I can still live again, I felt that I had turned to stone, and was no longer alive. I kept telling myself that, whatever happened, I must not cry before Mr Hewer, or before Mother when I saw her, I had got to keep a brave face on it. Then, in a voice which I hardly recognized, because it seemed to have lost all its life, I said, "That is cancer, isn't it?"

He said, "Yes, old lady", very quietly. He always called me "old lady" when he was really moved.

He started talking then, rather fast, and I knew that he was hating every moment of this. He would operate. He would take away everything that he could, and it *might* never recur. I hardly listened. I had had sufficient experience (even at that age) of people dying of it in the village, of operations which did *not* do the trick, of taking them puddings, and fruit, tit-bits and magazines, day after day, and then one day not going any more! Of a dismal little funeral into a church-yard overgrown with weeds. The end.

Oh, not that! I gasped to myself.

I asked faintly, "It – it is going to be all right, isn't it?"

"I hope so, one can never say, but I do hope so. I'll do my best, old lady," and he meant it.

I had the feeling that this was hurting him quite a lot, but it hurt me a great deal more. I knew enough about cancer to be afraid of it, for our village had so many cases. He said, at the worst, it would be all right for three or four years probably, and there were cases when it disappeared miraculously. He wanted me to remind myself of this when I got depressed.

"Where there is life, there is hope," but again, I had brought that one out frequently in the village, and knew it well.

He did his best, and I was calm and did not cry, but at the end, quite suddenly, to my shame, I flared up and said, "Why do we think that God is *good*? It isn't true."

He said nothing, but I felt that he understood.

He ferreted out some chocolates from somewhere or other, murmuring, "It's going to be all right, old lady," in that soothing way of his, but the "old lady" was *not* convinced. Years later when he visited me at my London flat, he said he had wished he could die that time, recognizing how frightful the news had been. He asked if I could get home all right, and I said, "Yes, of course," and then asked him what I should tell her.

"Nothing at all," he said, "pretend the report has not come through yet, and leave it to me to tell her tomorrow. But keep her spirits up; do try to realize that there are cases, numbers of them, when it never returns, for some strange reason. You *could*

My great-great-grandfather, James Bloom, painted at the time of the Napoleonic Wars

My great-grandmother, Frances Graver, 'The Rose of Norfolk', later wife of John Hague Bloom

Myself at 18 months

Myself, aged 8, in Marie Corelli's drawing-room in Stratford-on-Avon

be lucky. Try to think of that, and live today, without worrying too much about tomorrow."

I thanked him, and walked home feeling quite awful, as though it was not really me at all. In my life things had never been too easy. Perhaps the truth is that life itself does not play the game! I did not trust it. I tidied up and went back to see Mother. She was sitting up in a chair at the window, with the funerals going up the road to the cemetery (it really was the most *rotten* situation for a nursing home.) Later on, she told me that I had "talked like mad", which was probably true, because it was the only way that I could keep my spirits up. If I had gone silent, I should have wept, then she would possibly have guessed something.

I went back home to cook my brother's supper. I did not tell him about it yet, because I did not want him to worry, and I wrote a letter to my father. He came over to see me.

I was not particularly nice to him. I felt sure that he had added to her troubles, and some of this was the reaction from what she had suffered then. I had never hesitated to tell my father what I thought of him, and that was practically nil. Yet he could be such a nice man! It is these complexities in life that make it so extremely difficult to live.

I shuddered to think of how Mother would take it, for she had always been so compassionate to other sufferers in the village. She was, of course, quite marvellous. Her first response was a valiant attempt to cheer me up, and remind me that there were cases when it did *not* return. We must, she said, live today for today, and forget tomorrow. But there are some horrors which you cannot set aside so readily.

She had the operation and recovered wonderfully.

But now we had other problems. What about the future for Joscelyn, who was growing up? He could not stay on for ever at Wolverley School, where his reports were fairly poor. He and I had awful rows about them at times, because we had entirely different natures. If I had had the advantage of an education, I dare wager I would have gone all out to get top marks. If I was not the head girl, I would have been a most gallant runner-up!

Mother had harboured the dream that one day Joscelyn would

be the saviour of the entire situation, and when he grew up, would do wonders. I thought he had been too ill, and this had left a lasting impression on him.

Now money was desperately short. Mother felt that the solution would be to get Joscelyn home, and find a job for him. He was just old enough, but what could he do?

As ever, the solution lay with me.

I thought that a bank could be the answer, for he was supposed to be good at arithmetic – my own weak point – and I believed that a bank could solve the problem for us. They accepted boys of his age, paid small wages, but kept them to the end, with a pension to come. It was a life job, and this was what I wanted for him.

I got sick of dealing with big problems, but somehow or other I could not shake them off. When we were at the rectory, I had been friendly with a girl called Muriel Guinness. Her people had taken a lease of Ettington Park when Mr Shirley died and Evelyn had gone over to the Irish estate. I was always cycling over there to tea with Muriel. And the Guinnesses were bankers!

I wrote to Mr Guinness explaining the situation, and saying what my brother had finished at school, which did not take more than a line or two! He was now growing up, and I did so want to get him into a bank, but he was afraid that possibly they did not accept clerks who were quite so young.

I must say that Mr Guinness was goodness itself to me, and he wrote back giving me particulars of how my brother had to apply. He would go to London for an interview.

It was a horror to think that he might have to work in London, but perhaps we could find cheap digs for him. Also he would have to pass an entrance examination, which was a worse horror, for he had done nothing remarkable at school. But we had time, and Mother and I talked it over, and finally I managed to get a coach for him, which was not cheap. I sold the funny little bits of jewellery which I had collected as a child. I had a gold curb bracelet from Uncle Herbert, and the silver hairbrushes Mr Boyden had given me, also a little ruby ring of my grandma's. They were all silly little things, but I scrapped together the money. I bullied my brother over his coaching, I did not wish to

lose my valued knick-knacks, and then have him "play about" as
I put it.

He failed the first time, but got through the second. The bank
was helpful; he would be in a northern suburb, and they told us
of good cheap rooms for him (as the pay was £75 a year, the
rooms had to be cheap). We got him a new suit, and the things
that went with it, and I had not two shillings left in the end. But
once he was in the bank, I understood that he would stay, and
every young man has to be started in a career.

There seemed to be very little point in staying on in Stratford,
and we felt that we could do better if we went nearer to Joscelyn,
so that he could live with us. He needed home life, and then we
could save the money.

We thought of St Albans, where Mother's old uncle lived at
the Heath Farm. Uncle Jacob went there in the middle of last
century, inspired by the idea of supplying milk for London, and
he *had* done well! Also I had a young man in the neighbourhood,
whom I had met at a dance at St Albans' Town Hall, when
staying with my great-uncle. Montie, being an architect, said
that he would find us a good and cheap home, which he did. It
stood on the 'wrong' side of the railway bridge, in the Hatfield
Road, overlooking the Clarence Park. It was far better than the
awful little workman's cottage from which we moved, for the
Shottery Road had been the *end*!

This house had four bedrooms, one fitted with a bath (which
never worked) and three sitting-rooms with a pleasant little
garden at the back. This was how we came south.

3

MAKING ENDS MEET

The main work of moving house lay on my shoulders, for Mother was far from strong, and she simply could not be worked. The new place, being larger than the cottage, made it much easier, of course, but I was furious about the unworkable bath, and said so. We never got it put right.

The first real joy was to find that household shopping was far cheaper in St Albans than it had ever been in Stratford, which had always given itself airs.

One dare eat more, even have second helpings sometimes, and I, at the growing age, did find this an enormous help.

We spent the first night staying with Uncle Jacob and Aunt. They were most kind, but they strongly disapproved of the broken marriage, and thought that Mother had done the wrong thing. They abided by the old-time principle that marriage is for life, and it distressed us that they felt this way. We simply could *not* have gone on as we were.

I was still worried about Mother's operation. It was the constant ghost on our doorstep, and we *had* needed cheering up. We wanted a fresh start and new friends.

We moved in easily, and liked the place. Soon after that, it occurred to me that my father was not alone at Whitchurch. We had left him with a housekeeper and maid, and then somehow he changed it all. I felt apprehensive, knowing what he was, and wondered if he had actually got Miss Sims down there, to housekeep for him? In the end, he admitted with a chuckle that this was what he had done.

If ever a man played with fire!

We met in London, and had a long talk in a very noisy Lyons.

He said he had been obliged to find a home for Miss Sims when her brother turned her out, and putting it mildly, this was the cheapest way. It sounded awful to me! I murmured something about the Bishop, and he said there was no need to worry there, for that would be all right, and he giggled. I thought *nothing* of that Bishop.

However, he had had trouble, because one day when he and Miss Sims returned from matins, they found Miss Adelaide Marsh sitting on the roller waiting for him! She had never known that Miss Sims was there, and the most ghastly row ensued. Apparently Miss Marsh had come, hoping to stay on as some sort of housekeeper, and found the job already booked! My great worry was what the village would think. Farm labourers are shrewd. They can make two and two into four, just the same as anybody else. Also they know everything, and undoubtedly they had put their two and two together.

I thought it was quite awful.

I supposed we were in a mess, and the only thing that I could say was, thank goodness that Joscelyn was earning, and "settled for life," which was the way that I had put it. I blessed Mr Guinness for his kind help every day of my life.

I was engaged to Montie Thorpe now, and his income lay somewhere in the £120 a year range. He was kind, protective, someone of my own age to whom I could talk, and I *did* so need a friend. Also he had always encouraged my writing. At this period I was making some small pocket-money by writing little verses, which were suitable words for songs, and this was the only success that I had managed to obtain in the literary world.

It was Herman Löhr who had started the tremendous craze for the ballad, with that masterpiece which sold, sung and known everywhere. It was *Little Grey Home in the West*.

At Whitchurch an actor friend had come into what was euphemistically called 'the schoolroom' and had been interested in my verses. Mr Digues la Touche published several songs with my words, and I received gramophone royalties for quite a time. I wrote to other composers, and sold some verses: Theresa del Riego, Daisy McGeogh, and others, but it was a struggle to afford the stamps. This was the only method that I knew of earning a living, for my stories were an utter failure, and no wonder, seeing how bad they were!

On the whole St Albans was an improvement, save that we knew nobody, and did not get to know anybody. I found that the final split with my father had terribly distressed my mother, although she knew that it was the only thing that she could have done. I believe that privately she had been praying all the time that when he was alone at Whitchurch, and had few of the comforts to which he was accustomed, he would turn back to her and want us to be with him.

The detail she had overlooked was the fact that he was *not* alone at Whitchurch.

It was such a shame that we were so hard-up, for at one time the Blooms had been rich. The original family living at Wells-next-the-Sea in Norfolk, had been, I believe, privateers sailing under letters of marque. Old John Bloom was rich. My great-grandfather (his elder son) married the 'Rose of Norfolk' who was the illegitimate daughter of a farmer and a gipsy. I imagine the Rose was born in a ditch, and when her mother brought her to my great-grandfather's house, asking for money, he took the child instead and brought her up as his own. She spoke French, she sang, she danced, she was presented at Court. He left her a fortune, disputed by his people, and it was thrown into Chancery, that graveyard of too many bright hopes.

My father earned money by his books and his cataloguing and translating of old deeds, but he could never afford much.

Anyway we had got to St Albans, and Joscelyn's future was settled. He was to join us at the end of the week. I worked extremely hard to get the house spick and span for his arrival. Montie had got it papered and painted for us, so that needed no attention, and the furniture did look very nice.

I worked myself nearly to death in it, and Mother – who had felt quite ill with the effort she herself had had to make, and of course with her homesickness for Warwickshire – said that the house looked just as if we had lived there for a month.

On the Saturday, a little late for lunch, Joscelyn would appear from London, having paid up for his digs, and henceforward he would have breakfast early, go to Town, and come back in the evening, just like thousands of others. I had bought a season ticket for him. I did not go to meet him, for there was still a lot to be done, and I was making wild efforts to get that awful bath of ours to work, with which I had absolutely no success at all!

From the back window I saw Joscelyn coming down the Granville Road, and I went to the gate and along the pavement to meet him, for he would not recognize the house when he got to it. He was carrying a most expensive cineraria in a pot, which I presumed was his noble contribution to the home, and it would please Mother. Not for a moment did I think of it as being some sort of a sop, something which would pour oil on troubled waters, and how troubled they were going to be!

I thought he seemed a bit gauche. He was not at all enthusiastic about the house (and how I had worked on it!). Then came the awful confession. In the back kitchen he told me what had happened, standing there awkwardly.

"Look here" he said, "I've got the sack!"

For one long moment I could not believe that it was true. Mr Guinness himself had helped, and he was one of the big noises; what *could* have gone wrong? My mind flitted back pathetically to those little bits of jewellery that I had sold to help with his cramming. I had never even thought that this could happen. We stood there in the little kitchen, still in the process of unpacking, and I honestly believed that the bottom had dropped out of my world.

Joscelyn's ridiculously small salary, or some of it, was desperately needed for the new house. We thought he was going to be 'the lodger' in our lives, and supplement the measly income which was all that my father could afford to give us. It was going to be hard going at first, but bank pay went up almost automatically and we would have to have managed until that time.

I stammered, "But ... but they couldn't do that."

He did not understand how it had happened, for at school arithmetic had been the only thing he was good at. He had never done well, of course, but there had been the one occasion when he had won a prize, which had sent the family into ecstasies, until we found that it was offered to the boy who could collect the most snails from the headmaster's garden.

I stared at him. Then, after a moment, I said, "We ... we have got to tell Mother ..." and dreaded it.

She (poor thing) was horrified, because we had achieved the move realizing Joscelyn's need, and now his career as a banker was over. That night we had a long family talk, and we made him appreciate the fact that (whatever he thought about it) he had just *got* to get another job. He was, of course, far better working with his hands than his head; his hands were very clever, and surely, I suggested, something in the engineering line might be his cup of tea?

On the Monday morning he went out looking for work. Montie had tried to be helpful, making a few suggestions, but he had shown not the slightest surprise when he was told that the bank had sacked Joscelyn. He said he could not think how he had lasted so long there! I asked if there was anything going in his office with Mr Mence. He was quite firm about that one. There was *not*, he said.

Joscelyn returned home on the Monday, late for his lunch, but bright as a button, for he had already got a new job, and he would be starting that day week! Beyond the Clarence Park in St Albans, there were factories galore, and he had gone to the Sphere Arc Lamps factory where a Mr Hecht presided. There had been an alluring poster which had led him within to enquire further into the matter, and he had actually met Mr Hecht himself. He was one of those rather bossy little men (nobody liked him very much, and, being a German, less so when the war came) though his wife No-No was one of my best friends, and my bridesmaid when I married. Joscelyn had signed on for three years' training, which was the time required by the factory.

"Three years?" My poor mother could hardly believe our luck when she heard it, for here he could *not* get sacked.

I, by far the more practical member of the family, put forth the next question, with some eagerness, for I was the one who had to cope with family resources, and did I find it hard to make the money go round!

"What's the pay?" I asked.

There was no pay at all.

They were training him in return for his services, otherwise he would have had to pay about £500. I remember that I stood

there staring at him, with the feeling that I had been turned to
ice, for I really could not believe that this awful thing had
happened to us. But there *was* no pay, though in his last year
there would be some nebulous 'pocket-money'. He said that
when qualified he could get a good job, so it was a means to an
end.

To me three whole years seemed to be an eternity when
anything could happen, and probably would. I was so angry that
I flew at my brother and attacked him, and Mother turned cold
with sheer horror. How on earth should we live? The house was
more expensive than the one at Stratford, for we had relied on
Joscelyn's earnings. His contribution would just swing the
balance. Meanwhile the three of us had got to live, and every day
one has to eat.

That night in bed Mother and I had a stern talk together about
it all.

I had to talk her round to my own conclusion, and this was not
going to be easy. The truth was that *I* was now the one who
must take a job. She was dead against this, but if the pot was to
be kept boiling, what else could we do? She wept bitterly, poor
thing, for she had always fostered the fondest dreams about me,
believing that one of these days I should make one of those
brilliant marriages which get into *The Times*, and be rich, and
live happily ever after.

I must say that it did not look so much like a brilliant marriage
at the moment, for Montie had nothing, and anyway she did not
like him. Poor Mother! She was going through the worst time of
her life, possibly even worse than when she had had the courage
to leave my father. That had been not because either of us
wanted to do it, but we simply could not go on any longer as
things were, and we hoped that the shock would bring him to his
senses.

Women's careers were few, I could be a nursery governess
perhaps, but did not think I could do much in this line. I had
never had a scholastic mind, and realized this. I thought of taking
in dressmaking, at which I was fairly good, but Mother did not
like this idea, lest people came to the house for fittings, and she
did not think that she could bear that. Poor darling! She was of

the old school, and the time had come when life was going
forward rather rapidly.

Mr Hewer had warned me that it was a bad thing for her to
get upset, I did hate worrying her, so I let that one go. I'd do
something else, I said.

In the end it was Montie who had the bright idea.

He was extremely loyal, and I am sure that he was sorry for
me. He disliked my brother, and always had done, but I did wish
that he would try to conceal this slightly, for he let Joscelyn
know it every time! In his architectural offices, they were doing
a lot of work, for times were getting better and much building
was going on. Montie was a good architect at a time when St
Albans was expanding considerably. (His private hope was to
become the third partner in Mr Mence's office, when the hour
arrived. He said there had been a somewhat vague promise that
this might be coming his way; but nothing was certain.) His
family had, of course, worried Mother dreadfully, but now they
had sunk into the background a little. She, born in the middle of
the last century – 1860 – had very firm ideas about 'class'. I tried
to conceal the fact that the ironmonger's shop and the rather
indifferent home had not thrilled me enormously, and it had
worried me when his kind old father called me 'miss', so I got
Montie to stop him for me.

At this time the cinema was *the* thing.

New cinemas were springing up all over the country and
doing extremely well. It was said that the people who owned
them made a fortune out of them. Montie was busy putting up
one, that he had designed at Harpenden, which was the next
place to St Albans. Mr Clements from London had bought a
piece of land there, and Montie had designed 'The White Palace'
for him. The roof was just going on, when he took me over to
see it. Later on, when it ceased being a cinema, it became the gas
works show-room, and, as far as I could see, it was far better as
that than it had ever been as a cinema (but not for the world
would I have said so to Montie.)

As yet they had made no arrangements with a pianist, and he
was convinced that this would be just the job for me. It would be
something that I enjoyed, for one had to adapt the music to the

play, fitting it in at the right moments, and it was the sort of work that he felt I could do very well. I met Mr Clements who had originally bought the ground and commissioned the cinema to be erected to Montie's design. He was a little man with a pointed moustache, waxed at the ends, and someone whom I did not like very much. He had married a German widow who had a daughter, now grown-up, who had been born deaf and dumb. This was a tremendous responsibility for them.

Mr Clements was one of those little men who have worked all their life in the city, made some money, and now wanted to launch out into prosperity. He saw a fortune lying ahead of him in the White Palace at Harpenden, and I am sure he never got it for a single moment.

Montie was to be the manager, which would add perhaps another £2 a week to his job at Mr Mence's office. But the main trouble was that at night we should just miss the 10.30, and would have to wait for over an hour at the station before we could even start for St Albans.

I must say that it was no fun explaining this to my poor mother, because she just loathed the idea. In truth I think that she would have hated my earning in any capacity, which is perhaps understandable of her era, but the time had come when somebody had got to get down to it, and if Joscelyn couldn't, I realized that I could! What was more, I *would*.

There were bitter tears, a few rows, and then finally she agreed to it, and said that she would get a season ticket, also, and come over on matinée days when the hours were so dreadfully long, and give me a hand. Anyway she felt that at first I should find it a bit much, and how right she was! Naturally it worried me that she should be so distressed about it.

This was the time when cinemas were springing up everywhere. It was the day of Charlie Chaplin, Mary Pickford and Douglas Fairbanks.

The hours were terribly long. On matinée days (and when we started we had three of them a week) I had to play from two-thirty to five, when we closed down, reopening at six and going on till ten-thirty before I could thankfully crash into *God Save the King*.

I had to equip myself with a season ticket, and I left home at one-thirty on matinée days, but the real bother was the return home so late at night. The last train back to St Albans stopped at Harpenden at 11.55, and that was the one I caught each night. The exhausting day ended with an hour's wait at the station, where I sat with knitting or crochet, but the worst thing of all was that I had missed my meals. I sometimes got a cup of tea after five-thirty, but nothing more until well after midnight, when I finally arrived home, too tired to eat.

Anyone can imagine what my mother's view of all this, even though I *had* to earn, because we had not got sufficient without it.

There seemed to be no doubt that I was obviously the one who had to step forward and do something about it. In the end Mother did appreciate this, and always on matinée days she would come along and take over from me for a bit. This meant that I could get some fresh air, going out to sit on Harpenden Common for a short time. I paid her ten shillings a week, which was all that I could afford.

She was deeply worried that I got home so late, and unfed, and this was very trying. It was too late for a proper meal, so I had Ovaltine, or something like that, but whatever she felt about it, someone had got to get down to the earning of a wage, and it had come my way.

I wrote and told my father what I was doing, because I thought that he ought to know, and I received the most extraordinary letter. He felt that now that both of his children were "in jobs" (and heaven only knows where he got that one, for Joscelyn had no pay at all, as we all knew) and were growing up, it was high time that he cut down the allowance that he gave to Mother, for undoubtedly she had not got the same liabilities to meet.

When we got this letter, we were pretty well at starvation point. I should never have dared to have second helpings of meat or pudding, though I badly wanted to. I wrote him an extremely rude letter, and we both had a fierce argument. In the end I contrived to frighten him out of it, saying that I would come down to the rectory and have this out with him. Apparently he had some woman there whom he did not want me to meet, for this stopped the argument and he shut up. For the moment we were continuing as we were.

I never showed the letter to Mother. I said that I had lost it, and she believed me. I imagine that Miss Sims or Miss Marsh was with him at the time, because undoubtedly he did *not* want me there, and said that as I was so nasty about it all, it meant he would have to go on slaving himself to death on our behalf!

At this time Montie was an enormous help in everything and always my sheet-anchor. Mother did not like him, and my brother took her part about it, possibly because Montie disliked Joscelyn, and had, at times, been rather rude to him. I always thought that Montie had been provoked, but then I *would* take his side.

My start at the cinema was complicated. In designing the hall, Montie had set a balcony on the right hand side of the screen, with the idea of putting the piano here. It gave the pianist a most excellent view of the films, of course, which is vital, but what nobody had realized (neither Montie nor Mr Clements knew a thing about music) was the vibration which came from this balcony, and the echo it caught from the roof.

On the opening afternoon, with a special matinée, when all the élite of Harpenden had been invited, and special programmes actually printed in gold, I was not too happy about the way that the music went.

Naturally I was horribly nervous (far more so than I had been at any of my exams) when we opened with *God save the King*, and I was terrified that I would never be able to do it. The echo that the music caught was most disconcerting. Mr Clements was one of those men who live on their nerves, and he worked himself into a fever about this. It was then that I noticed that his nails were bitten down to the quick, a shocking habit of his. I told him what the trouble was, but he did not believe a word I said; then someone else explained that the piano *must* be downstairs, – even if Montie *had* built the balcony especially to take it.

The audience had complained, and I don't wonder, but it was very embarrassing for me, and I was too young to do much about it.

I did the matinée, got some tea and a queen cake at a café round the corner, and then started again before six, to continue until ten-thirty. I was never so thankful to play *God save the King*! I must say that I had never realized that wrists could hurt so much, and they had started to swell; at all costs I *must* get them right for tomorrow.

At home at the rectory, I had often done four hours' practice at a time, but that was a mere flea-bite to this. One had to rise to a crescendo when the audience were making too much noise, and try to drown them. I was new at the game, and knew nothing of that business which is called 'audience-control'. I learnt it, of course, and very quickly, but I was in a mess at the start of the first day, as anyone would understand save Mr Clements! The matinée had been by invitation only, so it had been a very composed and amiable audience, but with the evening show in came the 'rowdies'. They had trotted in to see the new hall, inspect it, and make a noise! Thank goodness Mr Clements caught an early train back to London.

It was two days before I could get the piano moved down into the pit, standing behind curtains where a theatre has its orchestra. Of course being so close to the screen, meant that now I had to crick my neck looking up all the time. The pianist has to keep his or her eye on the picture. But anything was better than having Mr Clements bullying me for something that I could not help. My neck hurt at first quite a lot, but I was going to stick it out; I should not be handing in my notice on that score with thirty bob a week at stake!

The music went well from this new position, save that there was one difficulty which I, in my girlish innocence had entirely overlooked. At Whitchurch I had never been bothered by pressing young gentlemen; in the orchestra stalls of the cinema, I *was*!

I was a fairly pretty girl, and the news got round. Their idea of drawing attention to their presence was, when passing the curtains, to make an attempt to pinch my bottom through them. They were not good shots! They had to guess where I was sitting, of course, and the one thing that they did not know for a time was that my mother sometimes sat there playing for me for a while, to give me the chance to get some fresh air. She was absolutely furious when they pinched *her* bottom! She took against this in a very big way, and told Montie that something should be done to stop it. This was all very well, but what could you do? The naughty young man would have disappeared before you could catch him, going out through the curtains into the vestibule, and after that, gone with the wind.

The more pushing of these people would send me in a box of chocolates (through Teddy) and my goodness! How much I wanted them! Scrawled across the box were the words:

"To the Pianist, with comps."

then the real gist of the whole affair:

"Meet you outside at 10.30?"

Teddy took them all back, and said that some of them used the most shocking language, which I can well believe. I was depressed, for I could have done with chocolates, and could not afford any myself. The whole thing upset Mother quite a lot, because she thought that it was dreadful! Her attitude about it all, was that a lot of common young men were taking liberties with me. Something should be done to stop it! My attitude was, how on earth could I retain the boxes with decency, *without* meeting the donor at 10.30 outside? But this I could not do.

Possibly the worst part of it all was the very poor arrangements that we had to make for my food. On matinée days, I left St Albans to catch the 1.45 and had had a good lunch but that was my last decent meal of the day. I had a short time between matinée and evening show, but tea shops were expensive, so I brought biscuits with me. We started off again after six, and I had to be there dead on time, for the people coming in like there to be some music.

I would often exist on a bar of chocolate until I got back to St Albans after midnight, when it was far too late to get a meal, of course. Mother always had a thermos of Ovaltine ready for me (then a new product on the market, and much advertised), and the doctor said this could supply everything that I needed. It was all very well for Mother hating my job (I was not too mad about it myself) but obviously somebody *had* to earn, and this was about the only thing I could do well. I never got a rise, of course; that would *not* have been our Mr Clements' idea.

My brother Joscelyn, aged 3, and myself, aged 5

Whitchurch church, where I played the organ (on the right of this picture)

Whitchurch rectory, Stratford-on-Avon

Montie and I always waited at Harpenden station every night for an hour, and what a long hour that was! He brought me home, dead tired, and only too anxious to creep up the stairs to bed.

At no time did I get any encouragement or thanks from Mr Clements, who from the first seemed to have disliked me, or behaved like it. He did once say that I had learnt how to stop the boys whistling fairly quickly, which I admit I had done. The pit was often a bevy of boisterous young men, who came to be threepence worth of nuisance. They would settle down to ruin one of the really big pictures of the day, if they were given a chance, and the main trouble was that when it came to throwing them out, they made such a row, and put up such a fight with Brooker the commissionaire, that nobody ever tried it, unless desperate.

The better-class audience sat at the back of the theatre, well away from the mob. It was the duty of the pianist to prevent, as far as she could, any disturbance of this nature, and not to let the threepennies "run away with themselves". Whenever the tune was familiar, they started whistling gaily, and what a noise they could make when they got worked up!

The thing was almost to encourage them, and let them whistle away, and in the middle, suddenly change the tune to something else, rather loudly. This had the most shattering effect! I was never the sort of girl who would sit down calmly, and not take action; I encouraged them, and then left them whistling the wrong tune and looking silly. They got to know of this, and were more careful, coming to the conclusion that they were the ones who looked foolish.

Teddy was the chocolate boy, and when there was a run on he lent a hand at showing people into their seats. Poor lad! He was such a very nice boy, a consumptive, and I believe that he died before he was twenty years old. I often think of Teddy, and how kind he was! Lovering was the operator, and he had another young man with him, but although they ran the show, nobody ever saw them. Brooker was the doorman in a smart new uniform, and he was there to come to my assistance if people became too troublesome. He was an ex-soldier and stood for no nonsense. One felt that when he was there, nothing awful could occur.

When the audience had a drunk amongst them, or some other kind of trouble-maker, Teddy called in Brooker — he prided himself that as he hauled them out, he always managed to bump their heads on the stone step of the doorway! They certainly got no mercy from Brooker, and although when I started playing I was sorry for them, I soon learnt my lesson, and the time came when I laughed at their discomfiture.

The cinema had a pit at threepence, the better seats running up to a box at the far end. Montie was proud of his design which included this box, though why he had put it in I could never imagine, for a toilet would have been far more useful, as we had none. I suppose that when he planned the box, he had had no sort of idea of the kind of fun that would go into it. Amorous couples booked it, and had no worry that they were so far from the screen that they could never see the picture properly. All they wanted was a good cuddle, and perhaps this had been Montie's idea. They booked it to have fun in it, and fun they *had*. However, there was one awful crisis, for a couple took the box, and were occupied with each other there, and somehow we had forgotten all about them. In the end, we went home and left them locked in the cinema, for Brooker had omitted to 'do the rounds', as he was supposed to do last thing of all. He said that he had thought that Montie had done it, but Montie and I had gone along up to the station, leaving the final look-around to him. I cannot imagine what the poor dears did. It must have been ghastly for them.

During this time my mother was working far too hard; in fact we both were. She was coming and going to the cinema all the time. She always gave me a hand on matinée days, and, if it was a specially big picture, she would come over again, about eight o'clock, to give me another hand with it. It was no help that she had always disliked Mr Clements, but understandable. To tell the truth, there was nobody in that cinema who liked him, unless it was the girl in the pay box, who, somehow or other, used to get on very well with him, and he gave her magnificent chocolates.

The rest of us never got a single one.

It had been very fortunate for me that Thornlea was so close to the railway station, for, if we had lived right up in the town itself, it would have been a terrible walk last thing at night. Montie's family lived on Holywell Hill, and he always said that the long walk was the last straw!

But to this day I am still haunted by that long wait of over an hour when I was already tired out at Harpenden station, listening to the express trains crashing through, awfully cold in winter, and so stuffy in summer. There we had to wait until the slow midnight train came along. Things are always easier for men, and Montie could go across the road to the pub and have a drink and a sandwich to go with it. I could never leave the piano, of course. There are still moments in my life when I hear those expresses thundering through. Montie and I would sit there, he with the money bag, I with my knitting, and I wonder how some thief did not find out about the money bag; but nothing ever happened.

We tried to persuade Mr Clements to get better films. He did not really mind very much what we had, and was a very bad chooser. I was the one who had the bright ideas, for it was I who chose *Sixty Years a Queen*, a risk, so Mr Clements said, but we had never had the cinema so full. There were several schools in the place, and the head mistresses looked upon this film as being instructive and booked whole rows of seats and brought their pupils along. We had to have an extension week for it, and I am sure we could have done with even more. I never saw the place so full, nor did we have a more attentive audience.

It was a glorious film to play for. I remember the end of it, the moment when the ship appeared in the Solent with Victoria's coffin on deck, coming quietly across with the crown blazing on that coffin. I remember turning on to *Lead, kindly Light* (only just a few bars to give the right picture of it). It was a proud moment when I got my audience crying, and their emotional reaction rested entirely on me.

After that big success, Montie and I pushed Mr Clements into booking *Quo Vadis*, which filled the cinema out again and again and we had a queue outside waiting for it. This sort of production demands a thoughtful and imaginative pianist to get away with it. Usually our programmes were very ordinary, but the big films asked for a real effort, and I loved it. I never cared for Charlie Chaplin. Of course he was wildly popular with the audiences but nothing very imaginative to play for.

The big success of a film depends very much on the pianist, who, if the audience is restless and difficult, has to make some effort to get them into a better mood. I liked that. I found that there was a great deal more to playing for the films than just sitting there strumming away. At the end of two years I realized I could get every ounce there was out of a film, but the effort was affecting my health. I had lost weight badly, mainly because I was going far too long without food, I am sure. I always had a late breakfast for I could not get up too early, going to bed so late, and Mother and Joscelyn had breakfast at eight o'clock. My lunch had to be early, when I was not really hungry because I had to catch the train to Harpenden on matinée days, and then would get nothing more, save some chocolate, or a biscuit, until about 12.30, when I drank the Ovaltine left out for me in a thermos.

About now, it did occur to me that I was not in love with Montie, but with his youth, his companionship, and the fact that he was someone who could help me in this way. At heart, I was extremely lonely. I liked the job, but could see nothing ahead of me, and I thoroughly disliked Mr Clements, who I am sure felt exactly the same way about me.

In the middle of it all, just when it was wearing me down, my father started being a trouble again. He said, and this was the good old story, that he thought it quite criminal that I was earning what he called "all this money", yet Mother said she could not do with a smaller allowance. She had the £2 a week, and he spoke of it as though it were a fortune, and said he could *not* afford it. I was indignant and wrote back from the heart. I suggested that Josephine Sims, and Adelaide Marsh, and a few others of his hangers-on, should work for him and help him out, as I was trying to help out *my* family. I knew that he had got somebody living with him in the rectory, but would never have admitted this to Mother, because I hoped she was not absolutely sure. Nobody in the village (and some of them wrote to us) said anything about it, but I still suspected that someone was there. It was so irritating that he could be so stupid; he was a clever man, but when it came to women he always chose such deadly dull and illiterate ones, and he went on doing it.

One day he came down to St Albans to see me, at a time when Mother had gone up to Heath Farm to see my great-uncle Jacob there. Dad at the time was in his more friendly mood, so much so that I warmed to him and told him of the eternal dread in my heart that the cancer would return for Mother. This for ever haunted me, but if I had sought help, I most certainly had looked in the wrong direction for it.

My father told me that Mr Hewer had said that there was far more chance of the wretched thing returning than there was of it completely fading out. It was the most unpredictable disease, and I gathered that my father was quite sure that it would come back. This horrified me.

I still think that he should never have told me. It would have been far kinder to try to pretend that she would be all right, and when Mother returned from Heath Farm, she found my eyes all swollen up with crying, and wanted to know what it was all about. I said that I had had a row with my father. It was the only thing that I could think of.

I did persuade him to continue with the allowance. He was always trying to take something off it, and it seemed ridiculous, for the living was over £300 a year, and he earned a lot with the work he did at cathedrals, looking after the deeds; also he was always publishing books. I had pointed out to him that Joscelyn did not earn a single shilling, and he was at the age when he ate a lot; so he certainly could not reduce the allowance. He was full of self-pity. Two grown-up children, said he, and he working himself to death for them!

We had had the most unhappy interview.

From his conversation, I gathered that he was still having affairs with different women. At this time, he was doing the deeds at Arbury, near Nuneaton. He never seemed to be out of a job; but then there were very few men of his great ability about at that time.

He had told me that recently he had met another attractive woman, and she had come to the rectory for a visit. I wondered what the village thought, for those people are very quick to take notice. He brushed that angle aside as being quite insignificant. He said that the new love did not approve of Josephine at all, and he giggled over it, almost like some schoolboy. I thought that the new lady friend was a nice one to disapprove!

I do not think that for a single moment he realized how badly he was behaving against all the laws of living life and of his church. In his old age, I know that he did change his ways, and then I was sorry for everything that had happened, and for the man who had made such a mess of his life. But at that time, Mother and I were struggling for help, and she was ill. I was losing a lot of weight. Sooner or later something would change it all, I felt, but not yet.

For the moment I had no help.

There is something most horribly demeaning when you are in the late teens, and having to discuss your father's illicit love affairs with him, though I don't know that this worried him at all. He thought they were "rather fun".

I did explain to him that we could not live on less than the £2 a week, and if he reduced it we could not live at all. I did ask, also, if he did not appreciate that he was a shockingly bad example to the parish. His retaliation was that it was not his fault that Mother had left him. I said that at any time the Bishop might find out something and have a shock; then my father would be unfrocked or something frightful, and we should all go down together.

He explained that he and the Bishop were good friends, and he had no fears along that line. So I gave it up. There was nothing more that I could do.

When he had gone, I sat down and had a good cry.

4

WAR DECLARED

It was that summer, 1914, that the First World War came to us, and unexpectedly. It arrived out of the blue, at a time when everyone was down at the seaside, holiday-making. There had been an enormous naval review at Spithead, on the principle of *God, Who made her mighty, make her mightier yet*, and none of us had the slightest idea that we were trembling on the brink of catastrophe.

At this time, the man whom I should eventually marry was an Assistant Paymaster in the Royal Navy, and was at sea. He would have seen war approaching before I did, even though my work at the cinema did bring me close to the news all the time. One lived with it. But of course Robbie was naturally much closer. The first mention that he made of the coming war is entered in the daily diary which he has kept all his life. It came on 28th July 1914.

We are under orders to sail at 7 a.m. tomorrow, at 14 knots. Destination unknown.

But it seems they woke up to the fact that something odd was going on fairly quickly, for in his next entry everybody was really getting busy. He wrote:

All the forenoon we have been preparing for action. Extra stanchions fitted round all the guns, and ammunition has been stacked in places under the turrets. Mess tables taken down to the bag flat. We have had orders to fuse all lights, but not to throw overboard unnecessary stores ... We made a dash through the Straits of Dover at full speed, with no lights burning. We had orders not to fire on any ship, unless fired on first.

From what he says, I should imagine that he was not over worried (as I should have been) and for the moment I think that the whole situation seemed to be exciting, a jolly good show, and something for a change! He was at the age when a bit of change is always fun. Nearing twenty-one, he little knew that this particular sort of a change can sometimes be too much of a good thing.

On 3rd August, he wrote again:

Apparently Germany has declared war on France, and on Russia. I should think it can't be long before we declare war on Germany. However, we are looking forward to war, to give us the chance to wipe Germany off the map.

It seems to me that the two sexes look on this sort of thing – declaration of war – in an entirely different manner. I had never thought with any enthusiasm of "having a bash", which was the way that Robbie put it. I saw the coming of war with a cold horror. It would change our lives, of course, and completely, I supposed, and it did mean that people would die. I was too much the parson's daughter not to wonder how the village would get on. Women would lose their only sons, and their husbands.

It is extraordinary how I am still influenced by my village background, possibly because it was there that I had been taught the wretchedness of human suffering, and had developed an extreme pity for the villagers.

Everybody said it could be only a very short war; we should eat our Christmas dinners in Berlin. They also said that Germany did not stand a chance, and oh, how cocky we all were about this! War would show them where they got off! We had the mightiest army in the world, we believed, and were invincible.

I was really disturbed about the soldiers in the village (we had four of them) and I knew that their poor mothers would be worried to death. My own mother was anxious because, having been educated in Germany, she was convinced that Kaiser Bill had got quite a lot up his sleeve (he must have been preparing for this for years) and it horrified her.

On Wednesday 5th August, Robbie wrote in his diary:

Nobody knows anything that is going on, and the Skipper won't publish any news that he gets. Declared war on Germany at midnight last night.

Even if the Skipper was keeping quiet, and they were not getting the news, I should have thought that the last sentence was sufficient in itself.

I was banging away at allied national anthems, playing them during the interval between the big picture and the news. The audience lifted the roof with their wild approval, for they were in that mood, and never had England been so patriotic.

Montie said "I hope the damned building stands up to it, but if we get too much of this sort of thing, it won't! Then what?"

We felt that the actual declaration had been a good thing; most certainly we could not keep out of this, and the suspense had been quite awful. We all wanted to fight, if only to show Germany where she got off! We would not have missed that joy for all the world. None of us thought that it could possibly last until Christmas.

The man who one day would be my second husband was having something of a to-do, for that afternoon apparently an incident did happen. I must say that even if the Skipper didn't talk, they were having a full round of fun in other ways. He wrote:

There was an awful spasm in the afternoon. One of the ships sighted two German submarines, and we went to action stations. We remained there for an hour, but we weren't attacked, and we lost sight of them, so we played hockey in the dog watches. I have the first watch tonight.

On the actual night when we did declare war, Mother and Joscelyn went up to St Albans Town Hall to hear it. Not for the world would Mother have missed that, even if it was a long walk for her to take, and very late indeed. She was wildly enthusiastic, and would have cheered like an eager child. They were still singing round the Town Hall when Montie and I walked back from the station to Thornlea. I was already sick to death of the sound of *Land of Hope and Glory*, for I had been at it in the cinema half the evening.

At this moment England was going mad with joy over

something which was perhaps one of the greatest tragedies that we were ever to know. They felt that we could at last get at the enemy, and show him what we were made of. I was not very happy. These nasty presentiments that I get so easily would not let me be, and I saw misery ahead. I remembered when I was a very little girl grown-up people telling me that England had never really recovered properly from the South African war, and I realized this to be true. I know that Mother told me that before that war you could get eggs when they were plentiful at tenpence a dozen, and I believe that too was true. They would never be that again. But at this moment England was wild with joy that the war was 'on'.

If I had ever thought for a moment that the war would not affect us all very much (for after all it was a long way off) I was entirely wrong. I soon found this out. The first bother over at Harpenden was Brooker. He was in the reserve, called up at a moment's notice, and he just disappeared. There we were at the White Palace with no commissionaire, and nobody to chuck out the drunks. Mr Clements was furious over it, but he was hardly in the position to talk, having a German wife and step-daughter.

At this hour, when every man in the country was joining up somewhere the chances of getting somebody to take Brooker's place looked like being fairly hopeless. Of course Teddy was too young and too ailing to help with anything like that. Also with the war coming, all the men often seemed to have been 'having one' to celebrate, and the cinema was thoroughly rowdy.

We had often had trouble with noisy drunks in the pit, and then Brooker would wrench them out of their seats, and through the curtains, out of the glass doors, and down the steps with a bang! This was *not* a woman's job, of course, and Mr Clements would never take a hand. Montie was slim, not very sturdy, and one really tight bricklayer would have been impossible for him!

What do we do next? I asked myself.

At breakfast next morning, we had a general family talk about the future. My brother then promised Mother that for the moment he would do nothing about joining up, but would wait and see which way the cat jumped.

Next morning, however, he did not return to lunch as usual, and we got a hurriedly written postcard which neither of us could read. He came to see us next day, having horrified my poor mother, and he was then wearing the most ill-fitting army uniform that I have ever seen. I think that he was a bit concerned about the sort of reception which he would receive, and it was not a matinée day, so I was at home, to add to his other troubles.

Mother was lying down at the time, and we went up to her bedroom to see her and to explain things. She was intensely proud of his courage, of course, so was I, but deeply worried that she would upset herself, and she *was* feeling rather poorly at the time. I left them to talk, and after a while I heard her bedroom door closing, and him coming out of it to the stair head. The thing that I heard next was the most appalling crash, for he had been tripped up by his spurs, wearing them for the first time, and had come the full way down the stairs, to lie sprawling in the hall. One would have imagined that this would have done something to squash his martial ambitions, but oh no! He was not even hurt, though Mother and myself were most concerned.

"He will kill himself in those awful things," Mother said. "Goodness me, what *is* happening to this world?"

That was what everybody wanted to know.

Joscelyn had joined up with the Royal Field Artillery and apparently he was now camping on some of the waste land which lay behind my great-uncle's farm at the heath. He said that there were hundreds of them there, and that the food was dreadful, because as yet they had not got into their proper routine. Yesterday he had had practically nothing at all. I gave him all the food that we had got in the house, whether we could spare it or not, and how on earth I should replace it I simply did not know.

Then I had to rush off to the cinema, leaving Mother weeping bitterly about it all; she was convinced that Joscelyn would be killed, and he was limping back to barracks, which was what the heath now seemed to be.

When I got to the White Palace there was little comfort there, for Mr Clements was in his very worst mood. This time he was really in trouble. His wife was German-born, and she had this deaf and dumb German daughter who had never been naturalized. Of course the authorities had been round, for they were rounding up all German citizens, and he and his wife were terrified lest this poor girl would be taken from them and put into an internment camp. I did deeply sympathize with them in that, because it was a shocking situation in which to be.

Apparently every German in the country was suspected of spying for the *Vaterland*, and when it comes down to facts, it is not at all easy to prove that one is *not* a spy, as I found later on when I went to live by the sea. Some idiot there came to the conclusion that Bloom was a German name (actually we were Danes) and that by coming to live at the seaside we were dedicated to serving our homeland in a nice quiet little way of our own!

Mr Clements had always been one of those men who do not keep their troubles to themselves, and he was now agonized over the worry about his family. I was in trouble, for I could *not* get hold of the Servian national anthem (the country was known as Servia then). With the news I had to keep playing various national anthems of the allies I had twice been up to the music shop that day, and could get absolutely nothing at all in this line.

Montie was late arriving that evening, for he had been to the recruiting office to see about joining up with something, so that I got the full weight of Mr Clements' tale of woe, just as I was trying to count over the chocolate tray for Teddy to take around. But when Montie did arrive he got Mr Clements to go home, where he said he was sure he was wanted, and we should get along all right without him.

It was a ghastly night, and when ultimately Montie and I got up to the station to wait for the midnight train, even that had changed completely. It was most dreadfully noisy. The nice porter warned us that it would be awful, and it was. There seemed to be thousands of trains rushing through, and all of them were full of soldiers. I said that I was very sorry for Mr Clements and that poor girl, it would be awful if she was dragged away from the only people who understood her needs. Montie said that it served him damn well right for marrying a German, and he didn't care a hoot if he *was* in a muddle!

We then discussed the problem of how we should manage without Brooker. At this time, we should never get another man, of course, for all England was enlisting like mad. Teddy was left to us, sixteen, but with only half a lung, and he lost his breath in a row, and could never cope with a riotous drunk as Brooker had done so often. We had three girls. One at the pay desk, and the other two in the cinema, ushering people into their seats. They ought to be all right any way, said Montie, for, whatever else happened, the one thing the country could *not* do, was to call up the women!

But how, oh how, did we get another 'chucker-outer'?

Then we came down to the hard facts of our own lives, for this war (even if it was going to be over by Christmas) was offering every one of us a problem. Montie said that whatever happened he would have to join up, and this horrified me. I did not see how I could continue in my job without him, for he had always been my most gallant defender in emergencies, and believe me, there was never a day when some emergency or other did not turn up.

I hated the thought of being alone in the power of Mr Clements, whom I had always found to be the most difficult man.

I suggested that Montie did nothing definite about joining up until we had got Mr Clements through this present problem with the deaf and dumb daughter, and the German wife.

During the week, almost every man one knew joined up. I took some money out of my post office savings bank account and went down to Mr Handley's shop, and bought in some grocery stores, for the *Daily Mail* said all prices would "soar", a word I very much disliked, and some of them would now go off the market. Food was still cheap. I bought two seven-pound pots of really good marmalade for two shillings and sixpence a pot, some biscuits at sixpence a pound, and eggs at a shilling a dozen.

Poor Mother was desolate about it all. She did not know what to do next, and she was not feeling at all well, which was no help. During the week Joscelyn marched off with his regiment (destination unknown), to some place where he would train. That upset Mother yet again. The long trail of the R.F.A. was

due to march past our house at ten in the morning, and it never
came, until the afternoon, when most of the men were looking
like death! It seemed that the rations had gone wrong again, and
they had had no proper food. Most of them looked as if they
would drop out of it. We rushed back into Thornlea, scooping
up everything that we could get out of the larder, bread and
cheese, cake and biscuits, and the pork pie intended for our own
supper. We had to throw these into the wagons, as they marched
past us.

The whole thing was most shockingly badly managed.

I did not know what to do, for Mother was so dreadfully upset
(and she was one of those women whom it took a lot to upset).
When they had gone, we went into the house again and she
collapsed. She had had too much. The newspapers had been no
help, for they had written glowing articles about "men marching
away to their deaths" and all that sort of thing.

We did not get a word from Joscelyn for a week, though I had
slipped a stamped addressed postcard into his pocket for him, and
begged him to send it as soon as ever he could, because Mother
would be so worried.

The first news of the war overseas was not good either; for
apparently Germany had been only too well-prepared, and we
had not. Eventually Joscelyn wrote to us from Livermere, in
Norfolk, where they had gone for training throughout the
winter, and oh, what a cold spot Livermere is! Mother wept
again; he had already had pneumonia twice, and she knew that
Livermere was one of the coldest parts of Norfolk, and he would
possibly get it again, and maybe die with it this time. It seemed to
me that quite a lot of young men were going to die.

At the cinema we were in a real muddle, and my position there
was becoming desperate. What should I do when Montie left and
I had no Brooker at the cinema? I had always had extra jobs put
on to my shoulders by Mr Clements, and being tied to the piano I
did not know how on earth he could expect me to do them.
Anyhow, I could definitely *not* do Brooker's job! I lost even
more weight than before. The first night after Montie joined up,
I had to walk alone to the station at eleven, having done all the

locking up, and I felt lonely, and very frightened.

"This 'ere 'en't right for you, miss," the old porter at the station told me, and that was true. It was *not* right.

Probably Mother had been brooding over this for some time, and now, when there was no reason for her to stay on in St Albans as Joscelyn had gone, she had a bright idea. She wanted to get right away.

From her experience at school in Germany, and she did seem to know something about it, this would be no short war as everybody predicted, though they had given up the idea of our all eating our Christmas dinners in Berlin, and now even said that maybe it would last a year. Mothers never thought that. She said that the Germans were a most methodical people, and they would never have gone into it unless they were fully prepared to see the thing through.

As it was now fairly obvious that I had worked too hard and was ill, we could not continue as we were doing. The moment Montie had gone, Mr Clements had had no scruples in pushing this and that on my shoulders! There was far too much work. I had to check up with Teddy's chocolate tray, last thing, take the money from the pay desk, record it, and cart it with me home for the night to pay it into the bank for him next day. It is a long way from the Granville Road to Holywell Hill where the bank was situated. Besides, it was not the right job for a girl going home with the takings every night, as Mother said.

Mother took action.

She had one of those sudden bursts of activity which she often got, and she went down to the east coast, which had been practically deserted now by people who were afraid of invasion. She went to Walton-on-the-Naze, a place that I had never even heard of, lying between Harwich and Frinton-on-Sea, with Clacton, six miles further along the coast going south. She was lucky in this, for she found an adorable house and she took it. Glowingly she told me that you could hear the sound of the sea from the drawing-room. It was Queen Anne, a remnant of the days when Walton had been fashionable, and had been visited by all the best people.

I admit that her description tempted me, but I was worried

about abandoning my thirty bob a week job (which had never increased however much extra I did). Mother said that now we had not got to keep Joscelyn it would be easier. Providing a home, food and clothing for him *had* been a severe strain.

Mother had watched my strength giving out. Maybe I did overwork at Harpenden. At any rate it *was* a strain, and it took some years before I really got over it. The work had been hard but the difficulties over getting proper food had been harder. I had been quite plump when I had started at the cinema, and now I was almost thin.

After Montie joined up it had been wretched doing that long, dark walk to the station alone at eleven at night, when the pubs were 'kicking out', and there was quite a walk from St Albans station home after midnight, although we did have the street lights there. Mother knew, of course, how extremely difficult Mr Clements had been, and she said that two years' working for him was sufficient for anybody.

She had taken the Saville Street house at Walton on a three-year lease. Anything could happen, she said (and it did.) We were moving down there this coming autumn.

My first husband, Captain Arthur Denham-Cookes

Myself at Frinton (*above* on my
wedding day)

5

GOODBYE, ST ALBANS

The people who had been so sure that the war would be over by Christmas, and that we should be eating our Christmas dinner in Berlin stopped talking! We knew that the Germans would bitterly regret that they had ever started it, but for the moment, in the first rush, they were doing unhappily well. Naturally we did not say so, for that would have shocked people. Of course we had been taken by surprise, but our losses were now quite appalling, and the Germans came marching on.

Mother and I decided to move down to Walton-on-the-Naze as soon as ever we could. When I told Mr Clements that I should be leaving, he did not show a single sign of regret. He accepted it calmly, saying, "Oh yes," and then changing the subject. I thought privately that if it had not been for Montie, he would have got rid of me before, even though nothing had ever been said. How he would get somebody else, I could not imagine, because it was not everybody who had the adaptive power to play for the pictures.

He was still having terrible trouble with the German daughter, for England, at this moment, felt extremely antagonistic towards Germans, and on the actual day that I left he had to go early because some violently pro-English resident had sent a brick-end through his dining-room window when they were having lunch there.

He was so full of this story that he forgot to say goodbye to me: certainly he never said thank you. I am sure that losing Montie was more than he could bear, and he was beginning to find the cinema a millstone round his neck, for he sold it only a few weeks after both of us had left. What became of him I have never known. The last time that I saw the cinema, Robbie drove me down there to have a look. It had become the showroom for the gas works, which was something of a come-down, so I thought.

Meanwhile we got news from Joscelyn, now stationed in Norfolk, which is not the best county in England in which to spend the winter, and this distressed both Mother and myself. He said that the food was downright awful, and the training an ordeal. It was one long tale of woe, and I expect it was rather ghastly after home. Mother was worried, for the last time she had seen him he had not looked at all well.

I thought that getting right away would do us both good, for we had not been too happy at St Albans, and now that Montie had gone we had no friends left. Uncle and Aunt had never been very forthcoming. In fact I had been to visit them only about half a dozen times at the most, and then I was not always too welcome I felt. Living under a cloud is a dreadful thing for anybody.

Our optimism about the war began to suffer. We had thought that Kaiser Bill would find that he had made a mistake in going into the war at all, and he would gracefully retire from it. Not he! Already many of our young friends were dead. Germany had got a terrific army, and it was extremely well trained. Some said that they had been 'hotting up' for this for ages, and he had only waited for his uncle King Edward VII to die, before he started the ball rolling.

I had played my last national anthem at the cinema, closed the piano, and as usual took the key of it upstairs to lay it on Mr Clements' desk. He had already gone home. I had rather hoped that he might give me a couple of pounds in gratitude for faithful services, but I am afraid Mr Clements was *not* that sort of fellow! There was a letter waiting there for me, closely sealed, which put high hopes into my heart. This is *it*! I told myself. But it was only to tell me to leave the key of the chocolate store in a certain corner of his desk, so that he would find it when he came in on the following Monday.

The programme girl said that as yet he had not got anyone else to play the piano for him, but was in touch with a young man who played the cornet! This did not sound as if it would be a success to me.

"He *can't* do that!" I said in cold horror to Miss Rogers.

"He can do anything, you know what he is!" And how right she was! I could not imagine what would happen to the cinema, but the girls did not seem to care. Could it be possible that Mr Clements thought he could run the show with just a flute, and no pianist? We had had moments when I had been backed by a flute, a violin and a 'cello, but that had not been too wild a success. They went one at a time over to the pub for refreshment, and then did not come back for the big picture, which was the end. I never liked the weeks when we got in extra musical aid, for this reason. They all seemed to be so much in need of refreshment, whereas I had to go on and on, very often with absolutely nothing at all to refresh me.

I walked alone up to Harpenden station to wait there for the last time for the midnight train, and I knew that I should never do this again. Perhaps in a way it was a good thing that this was coming to an end, for it had been a gruelling time and I admitted to feeling ill. I knew also that my buoyancy of spirit was just beginning to weaken.

I sat down alone in the dim waiting-room, to knit some khaki socks for Joscelyn, and as I sat there the troop-laden trains kept whirling through, going to the coast. Ever since war had been declared, the station had been horribly noisy at night. The trains seemed to be unending.

The porter told me that it had been like this all day. He was sorry that I was leaving, but he thought that mine was a rotten job, and far too much for any young girl.

We said goodbye quite affectionately, I almost in tears. It was then I knew how sorry I was to be leaving, as the train chuffed out of the station – for ever as far as I was concerned.

I got out at St Albans, and said good night to the man on duty (also an old friend) and then I walked through the yard, up those wooden steps, and over the bridge. Soldiers were everywhere, and even sentries gave a low whistle when they saw me coming along the road, up our steps, to set the key in the door. All this was *for the last time*. I knew that I wanted to cry.

"That you, darling?" came Mother's voice from the room above.

"Yes, it's me. I'll be up in a moment," but as I shut the door and locked it, I knew that I turned the key on part of my own life, because I should never go back to the cinema again.

In a great ship, the man whom one day I should marry, wrote, heading the entry in his diary with those two words AT SEA:

Had from 5 to 7 on watch last night. Glorious sunny day. Broad daylight all last night, rushing down the coast of Ireland at 14 or 15 knots all day. Had a game of hockey, and a double round the deck after tea. Didn't get dark until about 11.30, but it is now midnight, and I have just come down from an hour and half's walk on the quarter deck, with Wood. Had two rubbers of auction bridge in the afternoon, and two after dinner. Turkey declared war on us today, and we signalled it by occupying Cyprus.

I suppose different people take their wars differently but I would not have swapped places with him. Games have never interested me very much, perhaps because the whole of my life had been occupied with the village, rushing round visiting the sick getting things done for other people, which had always seemed to me to be far more important than playing games. I should have thought hockey and bridge dull as ditch water!

But that very night, as I locked the front door after me, and went slowly up that cheap little staircase to the room that I shared with Mother, I knew that my life, spent playing for the pictures was over for ever.

What would come next?

We got the furniture packed, and the big vans left the road we had known so well, and Mother and I took our own small bags and Juliet (the widow of Romeo the pug) to spend the night at Heath Farm with Uncle. It would take a whole week for the furniture to arrive, and we were going into rooms almost next door. I still hated to think that we had left Romeo behind us in the garden of Thornlea. I have always hated the finality of death: it is too abrupt; but this was not the moment to say anything to depress my mother.

Staying at Heath Farm was nothing like as easy or such fun as it had once been. Naturally I would have given almost anything to go back to the rectory, and I fretted for it, and to the very day when I write this, I am still at times homesick for it, but there was nothing that I could do to put this straight. We should never return to it whilst things were as they then were.

We had a nice supper at Heath Farm, and I always loved that comfortable bed in the spare bedroom, where my sister had been born some time before I came. It was pleasant not having to get up to get the breakfast. George did that. George was the parlourmaid who had lived for years, and actually died, in their service. Then in good time Uncle drove us both to the station and saw us off.

"Oh, I do hope that this is going to be all right," I said to myself, and instinctively I knew that the whole of my life was going to change.

I am sure that Mother was very glad that we were leaving and going to start again somewhere else. There was also the business of my getting engaged to Montie. She had disliked that too. I was fond of him, though of course never in love with him, and I did find his people very difficult, though his mother was kindness itself to me.

He had always been the most valiant supporter of my writing, and had encouraged me enormously with it, but the war was the last straw. He came home on leave, and then it was obvious that our feelings were cool. I broke the engagement off. We were to meet only twice more in our lives. Once, before he went abroad on active service: I felt that I owed him that much, so slipped up to London from Walton to meet him at Lyons' Corner House and have lunch there together. Later, after I became a widow, he wrote to me and I went up and lunched with him at the Trocadero, and I remember that I found it was surprising that he had ever meant so much to me. But of course this is what is so likely to happen to all young love affairs. Teen-agers are *not* good choosers on the whole.

The second chapter of my life had come to an end as we left St Albans for ever.

I hope I never see the place again.

6

NEW HOME, OLD WORRIES

We had to cross London to get to Walton, and go to Liverpool Street, a station which, though I did not know it then, I should get to love. It was pitch dark when we got down there, and by the coast they were very particular about no lights showing. I remember hearing the sound of the sea itself, for the shore was as close as that.

We left all but the hand luggage, and groped our way practically down the cliff edge, quite unaware that at that time there was no barrier, and one false step could have thrown us over the side. Mother had got tired now, and was weepy. She did hope that we had done the right thing in coming here. Privately I was worried to death about the financial side, because, whatever was said, we were very hard-up.

There might be a cinema at which I could play, I hoped for that, but was doubtful if Mr Clements would give me a good reference; he could be very peculiar about things.

The lodgings, which we had taken for a week, were next door to the new home, cosy and warm, with a pleasant supper all prepared for us, and that night when we went to bed we had the feeling that perhaps, after all, we had opened the door on a new life where maybe the sun would shine a little for us.

When I first went over number 15 Saville Street, which was the home that Mother had taken, I adored it. It was Queen Anne, built at a period when Walton was fashionable and famous people came down here to 'take the waters'. The place still bore the hallmark of this. There was no garden, but, as Mother said, without Joscelyn to give us a hand when needed, this could have been expensive and a bit of a trial.

I loved the little town, particularly in winter, for in summer it got crowded, and our trippers were mostly from what is known as 'the wrong side of London'. It had a straggling high street which ran from the sea itself, inland, ending at Walton Ashes, one part of it going on to Kirby, the other round the corner to Frinton.

It had the most magnificent lifeboat service, and, at that time, old Tom Bloom was the coxswain, a man with a gold medal. The first time that I saw them go out, I did not believe that any of them *could* come back alive. They really are quite the most wonderful men, and never get the admiration and the encouragement that they deserve. I think we all should see a lifeboat put out in a rough sea to get some idea of what it is like.

Now, in the new home, it seemed that at last we had the right sort of background, and that did help. The rectory at Whitchurch had been 'us', but living in digs had not been funny, and the cottage in the Shottery Road had been drab in the extreme. St Albans had been a rather cheap villa: it had no spirit in it; but Saville Street was quite another story.

But once again, here we were up against the old horror, for the bathroom did not work, and what was more, it never did. And that was a great disappointment.

However we had moved into what seemed to be amiable surroundings, and even if the wind off the sea was arctic at times (and, my goodness! *how* it blew!) it had a certain rather crude fascination of its own.

On the first morning after we had moved in, I was cooking kippers in the kitchen, when the dear old milkman arrived. I remember when he saw what I was doing (frying the kippers gaily), he said, "You're just ruining them there kippers, miss!"

I asked what it was that I was doing wrong, and he taught me. I give his information for all the world to read, for most of us have never cooked a kipper *properly*. It comes to you when you buy it *already cooked* in the kiln, and the only treatment that it requires, is to be submerged in boiling water for two minutes, and watch it swell right up! It makes all the difference in the world, and to this day I am thankful to him for teaching me the way.

We loved the house, and the furniture fitted into it so beautifully. At high tide, we could hear the sea, and when summer came, I would be able to run down to bathe. It was almost too good to be true. But on the fourth day there the trouble came.

I slept with Mother for the first week, for there was a lot to do, getting the place ready, and my own room (at the back) was taking time. Early in the morning, I thought suddenly that Mother was rather restless. I slowly awoke and got the idea that she was crying. Surely that could not be so? Both of us were in love with the house, and everything was settling in so suitably, even if the shopping was not quite so cheap as it had been in St Albans. I stirred and asked her what was the matter? Although at first she would not tell me, there came the moment when she did admit it.

She had found a little lump in the scar from the old operation, and instantly I remember sitting in Mr Hewer's consulting room, and his saying to me that it *was* cancer, and it seemed almost as if he spoke again to me here.

The wretched thing *had* returned.

I went cold all over; it almost seemed as if I lived through a lifetime in a few minutes. How right he had been when he could not reassure me that she was safe! It WAS cancer, and it had come back, and this was the deadliest enemy that we had ever had to face!

We had only just moved into an entirely new neighbourhood, and, as yet, we knew of no doctor to whom we could turn for help. For the moment, I felt lost, and quite hopeless, but whatever happened she must never know this, for she needed every spot of comfort that I could give her.

I talked to her until the daylight came, and the far sound of guns at sea with it. I tried to cheer her but both of us were sick at heart. I said all the usual things. "It may be nothing", "Lots of people get little lumps which don't mean a thing", "Don't jump to silly conclusions yet". Then I told her that as soon as it was light, and we had had some breakfast (which I would get early) I would slip out and find a doctor for her. I think that I did manage to cheer her, but unhappily for me, I could not cheer myself. I knew the worst already, and hated it.

We had come down here to start a new life, we hoped, and now the enemy was at the gate, threatening us. She meant everything to me, for I was devoted to her. If she died, I did not want to live and what could I do?

In my grandparents' time, consumption had been the deadly enemy for ever standing at the gate, the ghost which killed too many. We had, to a degree, conquered consumption, and today people were not afraid of it as once they had been. But life finds other bogeys to haunt us. The menace of this time was cancer.

The amiable fisherman-milkman told me of a doctor along the front, and when we had had our breakfast, a meal which neither of us really wanted, I went along to see him about it. I said all sorts of things to distract her attention from the horror of the moment. I talked hard, and I don't suppose that she believed a word that I said, but somehow I had to speak. Inside me, there was the ghastly feeling of intense shock. Time had elapsed. I had felt that things were getter safer.

The moment I could, I stepped out to see Dr Brockwell. It was one of those very raw days at which the east coast excels at that time of the year. I went on to the front, with an icy wind blowing off the sea, and how cold Walton can be! I found the house quite easily, turned in at the gate, and rang the bell. The maid showed me into the surgery in the front of the house, with that grey sea before me, the very long pier, and in the distance, still that echoing sound of gunfire.

Dr Brockwell is dead now, and it is unkind to say that he was quite the wrong man for me to meet at that moment in my life, but he *was*. He thought the cancer might have returned, and said, casually enough, "usually it did", and was entirely impersonal about it all. He would come round and see her, and he gave me a time, which seemed to me to be an eternity ahead. But he did say that there was a very good surgeon in Clacton, a Mr Coleman, who could operate better than any London man, and that did put heart into me.

All the same, I walked home feeling like death, and having to cling to the tamarisk hedge outside the Marine Hotel, for the gale was blowing hard.

I had the greatest qualms about leaving my mother in the hands of this rather callous little man, whom I had disliked on sight, possibly wrongly. And I was quite sure that he thought absolutely nothing of me.

He came round during the morning (and what a long morning that was!). He examined her, and said that the lump would have to be removed. It was quite a small thing that could be done here at home, but nobody could tell what it was until it was analysed. I'm afraid that that was no comfort to me, for I had had this one before, and I was convinced that it *was* cancer. We were back to where the whole thing had started.

He said again that there was this very good surgeon who lived at Clacton, and I could ring him up from the call-box at the corner of the road, and go over to see him as soon as possible. When he had gone, and I had comforted Mother a little (I made her have a whisky to stop crying) I felt better. I then went to the call-box and rang up Mr Coleman. He sounded utterly charming, and he was so nice.

"Of course you're worried," he said. "You come over here this afternoon," and he even told me the train to catch!

He, at least, was a dear.

It was most bitterly cold going over to Clacton that afternoon, and perhaps it seemed to be worse because both of us felt so dreadful. Mr Coleman was a darling. He said that one had to operate whether it was malignant or not, because no one wanted to keep the odd lump. It was better out than in, even if harmless. It was a small thing, nothing to worry about, and it could be done in the home. He said that we had got worried because it had been malignant before, but not every lump was of this nature, and if the worst came to the worst we ought to remember that today there *was* radium. He spoke of it with the greatest faith. We were, so we felt, standing on the fringe of the miracle cure, even if the malady was what we feared. He was most inspiring, the nicest possible person, and I am always so grateful to have met him.

I remember his asking me what I did, and I told him that music had been my career. He said it certainly hadn't been his. His only attempt at music had been one Christmas at the London Hospital, and he had been made to sing. Whilst he was singing a patient had died in the ward! He had never been able to live that one down.

He asked about my father, and I told him what I dared. It was so difficult to live with this kind of 'ghost story' behind us. He said that we ought to let him know, for undoubtedly he would want to come down and be with us.

I think, looking back on it, that Mr Coleman was really a trifle worried for me, because I was so very thin and pale. I told him that I had already written to my father (which I *had* done, and what a letter it had been but of course I did not tell the doctor that!)

He said, very kindly indeed, "You ought to have somebody with you; you are upset, and fear the worst. Try to forget that, for it could be absolutely nothing at all! Do take heart over that one! Get your father to come down and be with you, for he could be a help."

I must say that my father was very good about it, and most understanding. He wrote sympathetically, and said that he would come down, but would have to return for Sunday duty, of course, because although he had tried hard, he could not get another man to take the services. This was the worry since the Thrupps had left Alderminster, for dear Mr Thrupp had always been so helpful.

Meanwhile we got a living-in maid called Ethel, who was such a very nice girl, and it was a great help to have her here. She was doing everything that she could to be helpful, and already she and I were fast friends.

At that time, I did wish that our relationship with my father had not gone wrong. Originally I had been so very fond of him: he was a fascinating man, and very kind, but his schoolboy love affairs had upset everything, and it was even worse that he picked such very *odd* women. Certainly it had been very difficult for Mother, which I resented most bitterly.

There was a wretched storm on the night he arrived in Walton; there had been heavy rain, and it was cruelly dark. The sea was not in a good mood. To someone from quiet Warwickshire, the rage that the sea could show must have been most alarming, for it literally roared at one. I groped my way up to the station, clinging to a tamarisk hedge most of the way, for it was dark as pitch. I got to the funny little old station, which had never been altered since trains were first invented, and I sheltered in a doorway. I know that I prayed as I waited for the train. I was almost at the end of my own tether.

My father was at his very best, and most helpful. He was not worried about the storm, for he said that he had been used to this sort of thing when he was a curate at Harwich, and was only worried that I had troubled to come up to the station to meet him.

Walton is the most curious little place. It is almost impossible for a stranger to find his way in it, for it has so many odd little back streets, with humpy pavements, where one gets lost. Like Harwich, I think that when it was built, Walton was highly suitable for smuggling, which once upon a time went on gaily, and I believe myself, still does. After all, why should you not get this and that ashore without duty, if you can? To me it rather adds to the spirit of the life there!

The district nurse came to Mother, and she was quite wonderful and a darling. The operation was done; it took far less time than my father and I had anticipated, sitting in the drawing-room below, and listening to every sound above. Two days later Dad went back to take duty, and Mother seemed all right. But that night she came on with a violent pain. It was two in the morning, not the best time to run round Walton looking for help, and trying, in the dark, to find the district nurse's street. I went out in the most blinding storm, with a frightful gale belting round every corner, so that I had to hold on to something to stop being blown over!

I found her in time; she lived behind the station, and she dressed at speed, and off she went, I following; but she knew the way and got there with my key long before I did.

I staggered back as best I could, buffeted by the gale, and when I got in, I sank down on the hall chair and burst into tears!

Now all we had got to do was to wait for the result of the analysis. This was what had happened before, and I was not likely to expect anything but the worst. I must say that Mother had made the most brilliant recovery, and she seemed to be very hopeful and a lot better. But waiting for that letter was quite dreadful.

Four mornings later I had to go to Dr Brockwell again. Another quite frightening gale had blown during the night, but luckily the sea was not noisy for it was low tide. As I came round the corner, I saw on the flat smooth sand about twenty-five sailors lying in various positions, quite quite still. They were all dead.

Apparently the night before, a boat returning 'libertymen' to their ship had overturned in Harwich harbour, and they had all been drowned. Twenty-two of them had come in on the early tide, the others had gone out to sea, and would not come in for three weeks, when women would be ordered off the front, so they told me.

I have never forgotten the horrifying sight, and coming at a moment when I could not take it. I reeled into the tamarisk hedge. The Sea Scouts were coming down to help get them away, and there were carts passing by with union jacks over 'lumps' in them.

At that moment I *hated* the sea. "This is a ghastly place," I told myself, "most cruel," and I tottered on to the doctor.

That day, when I got home, Mr Coleman's letter came, for he had got the report of the analysis.

The growth was malignant.

Perhaps I had realized that it could not be anything else. Deep down inside me there had not been the slightest hope really, and now Mr Coleman came over from Clacton, and did his best to help me. He was really the kindest, nicest man we could have met, and, when he died, Clacton lost much that they could not afford to lose.

He wanted Mother to have a course of treatment at the Radium Institute in London. At that time it was in Riding House Street, and he had the greatest faith in it. I must say that all these places were awfully good to clergymen's families, for we were getting everything at reduced costs. They would give Mother a five days' treatment, and there was no pain attached, but some tiredness. Then she would come home for three months, and go back for further treatment. It might last for some time, for everything depended on how it responded, of course. We must *not* despair. That was silly, for radium was the great hope of our entire future.

Mr Coleman was the most tremendous prop to us, and we had faith in him. But nothing would move the eternal dread in me. I was quite sure that the black flag was up.

Our worry was affording this, for even at a reduced fee, staying in London is not cheap, and she wanted me to go with her. In the end, we found rooms in Gower Street, which at that time was the be-all and end-all for most parsons' families, because there were excellent boarding-houses. The cheapest sort were with cubicles, but, if you are poor, you have to accept this sort of thing. You may not like it, but it is all that you can get, of course.

There we slept in cubicles, with breakfast and supper, for nineteen shillings a week each. It was clean, quite comfortable, and with a good breakfast, though early in the stay I learnt that further down the street there was one place where you could get egg *with* bacon, not just egg *or* bacon! I wanted to enquire further into this, but Mrs Lawrence who ran our house was such a dear that Mother would not go back on her. In the end we always went there whenever she had radium treatment.

But of course I had been through a little too much. I was utterly worn out from the hard work, and the difficult hours at the cinema. I had broken off my engagement to Montie, and that had worried me quite a lot, for he had always been very very good to me. I had never been in love with him, I knew, but I think I am not the sort of woman who falls in love easily. The whole cycle of events had badly affected me.

I had lost a lot of weight, and had not got the strength left to eat a good meal. Mother naturally was most worried for me, and it was Fate which provided the answer. She had always entirely understood me, and was so good to me.

In spite of my pallor, I was still pretty, because the Bloom women do this sort of thing rather well. My great-great-grandmother had been known as 'The Rose of Norfolk' (which indeed she was) and I had inherited something from her. It seems that this likeness had been noticed by others, though I had not got a clue about it.

At the end of Gower Street, there stands University College Hospital, and behind it, the road where the medical students lodged at that time, and, believe me, medical students act very quickly. One of them had a mother who was staying with Mrs Lawrence at this time, and when visiting her he spotted me, and took the glad news back to University Coll. That day he stayed to tea, and came back to supper, and when he eventually left us, his mother said, "He has never been so persistent before. I can't THINK what has come over him."

I had no idea that it was me.

Then something thrilling happened. The hospital had a mascot called Phineas, who was a life-sized wooden statue, standing in the courtyard. Other hospitals were, I was told, jealous of Phineas! One evening, when some of the more ardent students had come round to the boarding-house for a word with someone, the warning rang out that another hospital had invaded Gower Street with the idea of "nicking Phineas"!

Out they shot, myself with them!

Now, as a little girl, the only friends I had were boys of my own age, and I was well accustomed to a good fight, but this was quite the best one that I have ever been in, and oh, what a scrum! I look feminine, and rather simple, but all my life I have been quite capable of hitting back, and I did. Mother, who had been trained with her brothers by the greatest boxer of all, Jem Mace, could do the same, and she had taught her children self-defence.

Gower Street was a seething mass surging up and down, first one side clinging on to Phineas, then the other, losing him again, then getting him back. In the end we *got* him and put him into his place outside the hospital. What a feat!

I admit that I returned to the hospital feeling a new girl, but an hour later, just as the dusk was falling (to make it more tricky) Bart's returned with a reinforcement from Thomas's. Of all the dirty tricks! we said, and out everybody shot again, myself amongst them.

This time, when we did get Phineas back (and that *was* a scrum if ever there was one), he was damaged. Also news of what was going on had got into the offices of the powers-that-be at University College Hospital, and they were hardly enthusiastic. The order went forth that now Phineas must not stand *outside* the hospital, but must be brought inside, where nobody could get him, even if they had the nerve! I must say that when it came to sheer guts, the medical student was a very good fighter, as I had found.

It seems to be quite ridiculous that a free fight in a London street should have helped me quite as much as this one did! When you are fighting in a whirl like that, you have no time to think of your personal difficulties. I actually rejoiced in the fact that there had been one or two minor casualties on the other side, and they had shown the greatest dislike of being brought into what they dared call "some unknown hospital" for treatment in 'casualties'. I believe they were extremely rude about our first aid (I had got as far as calling it "our" first aid now), so one of my co-fighters told me, but I am quite sure they got back as good as they gave!

But it was in that fight that suddenly I found my own girlhood again, and possibly Mother had known it would happen, and that was why she had not been worried for me when I shot out of the boarding-house to join in. It was the very thing that she had wanted to happen!

I hated going back to Walton after that. Three weeks later, two of the University Coll sudents turned up for a week-end there. Suddenly it seemed to me that, in spite of everything, my life was changing.

The Radium Institute had been extremely kind, and they were always most encouraging. They admitted that this form of cure was only in its beginning, but they were enormously encouraged by the results so far, and saw a tremendous future ahead for it. I am dismayed now, when I realize that all these years later, it has *never* done what they had so hoped it would do for them, and, even today, we are still groping in the dark for a cure. They tell me they are far nearer to it, but are they? I do not see it. But at that time both Mother and I were comforted, and that was important. We both returned to Walton from that first visit feeling considerably happier about the whole malady than we had felt when we had set forth. We know now that the thing to do was to live today for today, and not to try to see too far ahead into the future. At this time Mother was in no danger, and Mr Coleman, who believed implicitly in radium as being the answer, reassured me on this point when he came to see Mother on our return. He thought the strong sea air would help her, and anyway the conditions under which we were now living were far more comfortable than they had been since we had left home. (The rectory was always home to me.)

But very soon my father was in trouble again.

I came to the conclusion that he was a man who would never learn, and somehow or other Mother and I did not seem to be able to live ordinary lives at all. The Bishop had got busy. He wanted us to return to the rectory, and hinted that if my father was to retain the living, then we ought to go back. My father came down to see us about it, bringing a magnificent pork pie as a peace offering, which immediately made me suspicious that things were going to be more than a trifle difficult.

In the course of conversation he admitted that the affair with Miss Sims was still 'on'. She had had great trouble with a narrow-minded brother who was a draper in Bath, and because she would not give my father up, he had turned her out of his home. After a little questioning, Mother found that she was living in the rectory with him, ostensibly as housekeeper, and for the first time Mother actually realized it. I think she had always tried to blind herself. It seemed to be impossible for him to recognize that the position was so difficult, and to me he seemed to have lost all connection with life itself. How could Mother and I live there with her?

"You'll find her so nice," said he.

I suppose that I was older, so I laid down the law; in no circumstances would we possibly go back whilst Josephine Sims was there, and that was that. But the awful part was that if my father lost the living, we should have no income at all, only a few pounds a year left to Mother by my grandma, and then what should we do?

I took him on one side and told him that it was high time that he stuck by his marriage vows, and stopped being what he called 'kind' to other women, and always giving us such dreadful problems to settle. He said that I was rude. I think he was possibly right there, but I had got something to be rude about. I asked after Miss Marsh, and one or two others I knew of, and apparently he was keeping in with the whole lot of them, and they were "ever so nice" to him.

I am sure that he returned home slightly dispirited, and it seemed hard after the magnificent pork pie that he had brought with him, but what *could* one do? How he got out of that nasty situation, I shall never know, but he was a genius at getting out of things. Possibly the Bishop realized that most certainly he did owe my father a debt, for he had stepped in and had saved the church from the most awful row over the Portmans when they had come to Alderminster, and Mr Thrupp had refused them the Sacrament. My father had absolutely saved the situation, and even bishops have memories.

But, of course, all the time there lay this wretched basis of uncertainty. We never quite knew when a row was about to blow up. My father was never out of some sort of trouble (and usually it was the *same* sort of trouble) so that at moments we were worried to death.

Mother had recovered well from the January operation but she did find the radium treatment extremely tiring, and had to rest a great deal. I think now that, although nothing would have made me admit it, I was only too well aware of the 'dark stranger' being with us, a shadow lying, as yet lightly, across the path, someone, one never saw or actually felt, but who never went away.

This is a dreadful apprehension. Death takes up his residence; one tries, quite hopelessly, to ignore him, but he still is there all the time.

The troops (The Queen's) came to Walton.

It had now become quite certain that, whatever we had thought about eating our Christmas dinner in Berlin, this was going to be a long war, and nothing like as easy as everybody had believed at the start, when we had talked glibly of "one huge battle, and then the whole thing would be over with Germany wiped out for ever, and serve them right". But that was idiotic! Unexpectedly Germany had done far better than anyone had thought to be possible, for they had worked on through a quiet winter, and then had got ready for an uproarious spring. What our soldiers had suffered was unbelievable. By the new Whitsuntide, we knew that we were dug in for a long war, and that already the flower of England had perished for it.

Because Mother and I were two women living alone, we could not be billeted. Even if we had several empty bedrooms and would have loved the money this was not permitted. I went the rounds playing the piano in canteens, where they wanted an able pianist who could play almost any tune that she was asked, and stick out an evening doing this.

The man who organized this was Captain Bee. He was in his thirties and had a charming wife, and finding that I could play, enlisted my aid. Then he asked us round to his house for dinner one night. In those days, we had not yet outgrown the pre-war rather grand dinners of several courses, we were not properly used to wartime conditions; I brought out the sewing machine and smartened up Mother's dress and my own.

I remember that when we got there, there was the sound of distant gunfire at sea; we were rather used to this by now, and we got a lot of it. I knew there had been a fairly violent explosion quite near that very morning. I wanted to ask about it, but this was not done. In wartime you never asked any soldier about his job. He was supposed to get on with it in silence.

It was a wonderful dinner, with one guest absent, a young Lieutenant, Mr Denham-Cookes, who happened to be what was then known as 'officer of the day'. The nephew of Lord Lurgan, he had joined up with the Irish Guards, but had been kicked out, because (like Evelyn Shirley, who was his cousin) he had been born with a crushed left hand. I said that I knew all about that one, for Evelyn had lived near us. He was a very rich young man with an "awful old mother", they told me, who had married a very old man (dying soon after), and she had brought this poor young man up extremely badly.

But, they said, he was getting his leg loose now, and really enjoying the war! He would come in when he had done the final job of the day, which was to go to the end of the pier and back. This is a good mile, for Walton pier is second in length to Southend, and it is NOT a nice place for a walk on a cold windy night, when the world is blacked out.

On that very night, Robbie wrote in his diary:

Sea – Rosyth.
Got back to harbour in a roaring gale, at 9 p.m. and proceeded to coal. Just completed walking up and down the quarter deck, 32 paces each way.

I should imagine that this was dullness personified, and I had always thought that the sailors had such a gay time, far better than the soldiers did. Maybe I had been wrong.

At this moment, though I had no idea of it (perhaps you never know when the big things happen), my future was taking a new shape, and changing its course, but it was some years before the gentleman walking up and down the quarter deck, "32 paces each way", would ever know about me.

What a joy it was to sit down to a really good meal, and eat as much as you wanted, without having to leave something over for supper! Too frequently I had had to fill up with just bread, and, believe me, you get a bit sick of it!

After the meal, we went upstairs into the drawing-room. It was the era of the upstairs drawing-room, one of those tall houses near the station at Walton, with quite handsome rooms, and the drawing-room was indeed very pleasant. We had started the sing-song round the piano, with Lieutenant Denham-Cookes came in. He was off duty at last.

I knew him by sight, a fair-haired young man, not good-looking, because he had such a very bad skin; but he had the most amused laughing blue eyes, which could be quite enchanting. I realized immediately that he was shy, and not in the least 'girl-minded'. I gathered that his father had died when he was about four years old. The old man must have been over seventy, for the son was the child of a second marriage, and the old boy had fought in the Sikh campaign, I did not know much about history then, but I reckoned that was quite a time back!

The others had told me that his mother was quite mad, enormously wealthy, living in Prince's Gate in London, and that he had "the most awful sister".

His hand was covered by a glove, but I realized instantly that it was just the same as Evelyn's had been. Apparently his mother had gone down to Ettington when she was pregnant, and this had been just after Evelyn was born. She had been very shocked about the deformed hand, and frightened by it, and it had got on her nerves. Others said that there was a curse on the family, and it came out this way. The rumour was that Lady Lurgan had been R.C., and to marry Lord Lurgan had turned C. of E. I don't suppose that was true either, and my father laughed about it. I remember his saying, "If you are C. of. E. blame everything on Rome. And if you are R.C., blame the lot on the poor old Protestant. This is the way that the world goes round."

I must say that I liked Denham immediately, and thought it odd that a man who was not good-looking, could come from such an extremely good-looking family. (Lord Lurgan himself was a dream, as I was to find later).

We got on very well that night. I found that he had published some music, could play the piano, (even with that dud hand), and he laughed and said. "I do the bass all wrong, of course, but know how to cheat rather well!"

Next morning we met in that funny little High Street in Walton, which wanders inland from the sea. He spotted me, and to my surprise came across the street to speak to me. I had been out buying 'broken biscuits' – which were sold at half the price of the whole ones –, as we had to 'shop cheap'.

General Stevens was with him, a regular soldier, to whom he had apparently been *aide de camp* for a time. Now Denham was appointed to the Queen's. The General was spruce, he had an eye for a pretty face, and he liked me. Denham told me privately that ne was a most difficult man to please (I could well believe it), and I would not have been his *aide* for anything in the world. At the time (though of course I knew nothing about it), he had pounced on myself as being the most suitable wife for Arthur Denham-Cookes. Much later, Arthur told me he had said, "She has got both her feet on the ground in spite of that pretty face of

hers. She can keep a promise and does not go back on her word."
These were the things which would have appealed enormously
to him, and they happened to be quite true. How he found out, I
shall never know, but he *knew* all right.

Denham asked Mother and myself to dine with them at the
Albion Hotel where he was billeted. Mother accepted. Out came
the old sewing machine again, it was a game old machine. My
baby clothes had been made on it, and I was to make my own
son's clothes on it when the hour came. Denham sent the car
round for Mother and myself, and I remember noticing that his
chauffeur looked what I would have called "sort of funny" at
me, as I got in. That glance told me that the servants had begun
to talk. I don't think it interested me too much. I was only rather
delighted to be making some new pleasant friends, and going out
to dinner.

I was slowly recovering from the hard pressure of work that I
had endured at the cinema, and we could afford a little more
food, which was a blessing. I never heard anything from Montie;
he seemed to have disappeared, which I was sorry about, for I
like to keep my friends. Nor did I know how the good old
White Palace was getting along without me at Harpenden.
Joscelyn had been moved with his regiment out to Egypt, and
that had been rather horrible. He had spent the most ghastly
week, which was known in those days as 'embarkation leave'.
There is behind it the dreadful feeling that maybe we shall never
meet again, and, however you try to forget it, that keeps
cropping up.

Mother was wretched, and got very low over it. She had the
dismal impression that she would never see Joscelyn again, and
there was little that one could do to comfort her in this. On the
whole, she seemed to be better than she had been, and Mr
Coleman was convinced that the radium was 'doing its stuff', but
she still needed a lot of care. Every few weeks we returned to the
boarding-house in Gower Street, where Mrs Lawrence reigned,
and did another 5 days at the Institute (the most terrible strain on
the purse even though they were so helpfully kind with their
fees.) Mr Pinch, who was the surgeon there, was the nicest man.

The dinner at the Albion was fun. We got a really good meal, which was something. The General was in his best mood, and Denham quite gay.

Of course we knew few people in Walton, but there were few to know. Almost all the houses were taken by people who let rooms in the summer. Mrs Knocker from the vicarage had called. She was not exciting, a pale thin woman, and although we went to church there we did not find Mr Knocker a very convivial person. But we knew that Bloom was a German name, even though their own lifeboat coxswain bore this name, and for generations Blooms had lived in this town.

Looking back, one has to realize that when the first war with Germany came, people were abusively and violently unreasonable. I remember my horror when a small dachshund was stoned to death in the street because it was German. It is hard to believe that people could act in such an extraordinary manner.

Some busybody in the town wrote to the authorities saying that he thought we were German spies, and we were under suspicion. It was the sort of thing I had never even thought could happen to anyone. It was made worse, of course, by Mother offering her services in interviewing German prisoners brought ashore, because she was expert. They never availed themselves of her services, but somebody wrote to the authorities and said that we were "under suspicion". What had brought us to the coast at the start of the war, they would like to know. How did Mother speak such fluent German? In the end it got to the C.O., and I must say that he did not believe a word of it, and acted extremely kindly.

One evening Denham rang up and asked if he could come in for a drink. Round he came, of course. He expressed the greatest interest in the house, and invited himself to see over it. I took him even to the top floor with the wonderful view across to Harwich, and the backwater. He was very nice about it, and in the end I took him to the rather rotten little kitchen. I remember there was something lying on the side, which I picked up to throw away, and, as I went to the back door, he put out his good hand to stop me.

"Don't go out! Don't touch that door!" he said, and it was almost an order.

Amazed, I stared at him. "Why ever not? It's just the back door."

He said, "No! Do what I say," and bundled me into the dining-room beyond. I was most surprised, rather annoyed, and said so.

What had really happened was that he had been chosen by the C.O. to search the house. It meant that we had an armed guard at every exit, with orders to shoot if anybody tried to escape. One could not have believed it. My piece of paper for the dustbin, might have been misunderstood. Denham was trying to do it so that we did not guess a thing about it, which was very nice of him.

Denham did remarkably well, I must say, and most days he came round to our house for coffee, or a cup of tea, or a chat. Mother was enchanted.

I understood that he very much disliked his sister Kitty, and when I saw her, could well believe it. She really was one of the most stupid women I have ever met. His mother, known to my horror as 'Ma', was a real tartar, and he said that the army was the first time in his life that he had ever managed to get away from her! Even when he had been at Trinity Hall, Cambridge, she was 'after him' all the time. She gave him a pound a day pocket money and was always threatening to cut this off; he was afraid lest she would do this, and what could he do about it? He had so little otherwise to spend (only about £2000 a year and his pay). To me it sounded like unbelievable riches! Oh, what I could have done with it!

Of course to me it was inconceivable that anyone could ever spend a pound a day, for we were living, all in, on under three pounds a week. One had to go a bit short at moments, of course, but as long as Mother got better nothing mattered.

The year 1916 came in with a dinner at the Albion. We had a bad storm during the afternoon, with waves pounding over the sea wall and on to the street right along the front. I was now learning how dangerous the sea could be, and what an enemy.

From Robbie's diary, the new year came in in a somewhat jolly fashion, whilst I dined with Denham and others at the Albion Hotel, and drank to peace.

Rosyth. 31st Dec. 1915.

À busy day and a wet night. The Commander allowed us unlimited lights tonight, and we all sat up making an awful noise until midnight, when Martin rang sixteen bells. Then we all came down to champagne and sardines. The Commander (N) and Noel assisting. It is now one a.m. first of January 1916. The half-yearly promotions are just out, but the Commander is not there. He has always been known as the rudest man in the Navy, so perhaps that's it.

It rather reads as though he was pleased that the Commander was "not there".

At the Albion, we drank to the end of the war, and we all felt that surely it *must* end this year, because already it had lasted far too long, and we had lost the very best of our manhood. Yet it still dragged on and on. There would be even worse to come. I must say that the old Hun did leave us alone on Christmas Day, though he made up for that soon afterwards.

I remember the grim horror that came in the gloom of a January evening, with the daylight fast fading, when suddenly there came the most ghastly echo of gunfire (and far too near) from the sea. I thought that every one of our windows would be broken, and the whole house shook. I admit that our fleet, or part of the fleet, missed no time in coming shooting out of Harwich (I shall never forget how fast they came, nor what they did, the second that they got within range). For a moment I thought that we should all die, here and now, and there was somehow the feeling that one would rather have it this way than go on as we were doing. Mother, who was sitting by the fire, was not in the least alarmed, for she was one of those women who have never been frightened in their lives. But she *was* annoyed.

"Somebody ought to stop this!" she said, with mild reproach, "I think that it is disgraceful!"

The noise of gunfire increased, or so it seemed. Lying awake in the early mornings, one was always conscious of the grumble of far-away guns, and I was told that this was the echo of the guns in France. In the deathly silence of the night it was clear and quite horrible, knowing what those guns did.

Then the air raids began.

The wardens tightened up on the black-out, and all of us must have been quite mad, for, when the Zepps came over, we spent the evening sitting on the doorstep, so that we could be quite sure that we missed nothing! Thank goodness they missed us! One night they did give Harwich hell, I must say, and there came a long quivering sheet of flame along the horizon on the far side of the backwater.

On the whole, nobody thought that the war was doing very well. The Germans had achieved far too much, and had done *too* well, in the first months of the war, and I was convinced that we had been entirely unprepared. Older people did not accept this summary of the affair. It was very wrong of me to think these things, but most of us who were younger, did think that we had been caught napping. Far too many of our best young men had died for practically nothing, and if only we had known it, it would all happen again in a few years' time.

Our personal trouble was the continual agony of rising prices, for they were going up all the time. Once more I had to bar all second helpings for myself, for, whatever happened, Mother must have sufficient. I shall never forget that grim silent enemy, poverty, who stood for ever in our background, and even today, I shrink back from paying for something, lest I cannot afford it.

When we had friends to tea I bought stale sponge cakes at half price, re-heated them, and then iced them, so that they could be passed off as something quite delicious! I trusted that no one would ever discover the trick.

At this time my father was keeping fairly silent. Now and then he made an occasional outburst saying that he was giving us far too much, and how hard it was on him! We knew from letters which the villagers sent us, that Miss Sims was still living there with him, as some sort of a housekeeper, but I knew that everybody knew perfectly well what her position really was. Mother was not gaining strength, I thought that she tired more easily, and the sojourns with Mrs Lawrence in Gower Street, and attention at the Radium Institute seemed to exhaust her very much. But radium was the only cure − if it *was* a cure −, but there were dreadful moments when I went alone to the sea and had a good cry.

Sometimes I confessed to myself that it did not pay to pray for something. I had prayed so hard for Mother's life, but very little help had come. A friend once said to me, "Yes, I know, help does come, but it comes in a shroud." It is a horrible thought, but I am not at all sure that she had not got something there.

In the May of 1916 there came a spurt of the most glorious summer weather; it was one of the best Mays I have ever known. It seemed also that the gunfire was further off, and I bathed three times every day. The house was so close to the sea that I could run across a piece of rough ground to the Albion breakwater, a very treacherous breakwater with deep water on one side. I brought in two children from it one morning when there was a difficult tide.

I had the feeling that something was going to happen. One beautiful afternoon it did.

It was late afternoon, when tea was over and the washing-up done, with a couple of hours before dinner, when Arthur Denham-Cookes walked into the house. He asked if he could have a talk with Mother. She had had rather a bad day, and I told him this. He seemed surprised. I found that, until now he had never been aware of the fact that she was an invalid, and he expressed regrets. But he *did* want to have a little talk with her, if he could.

"I promise it won't upset her. At least I hope it won't," he said.

I went upstairs. She had been lying down and had had her tea on the bed, and she came down that beautiful staircase into the hall. Then she went into the drawing-room, shutting the door behind her.

I did not know why, but quite suddenly I wanted to cry! There came the extraordinary feeling that the world was going to change for me, and for no reason that I could think of. It could have been premonition, which has always played a big part in my life. I went into the dining-room, and stood there waiting under the pastel Mrs Canning had done of me when I was ten years old, a little girl in a sun-hat made of lace, and a blue dress. I remembered that I had been very worried when I sat for it, and I thought now, how much more worried I would have been if I had known how life would turn out for me. It had not been all beer and skittles, as Montie had once said.

I saw a telegraph boy coming to the back door, and pulled myself together in a momentary panic. In war time one dreaded telegrams, because one associated them with the casualty lists. *The War Office regrets to inform you* ... were the words I feared, for instantly I thought of Joscelyn. But this was a new boy who had made a mistake in the address, so I cheered up again.

Surely Mother and Arthur were being a long time, and what on earth were they talking about? Lately I had thought that he was fond of me, though he had never kissed me, and I also knew that his mother was jealous of me. He told me she was highly suspicious of every girl whom he met. She was apparently always threatening to stop his allowance, and thus frightening him to death, for he was an extravagant young man, who spent wildly (he had always been used to this) and I gathered that he was eternally running short. He entertained freely, and he had some friends whom I strongly disliked for sponging on him so vilely. They were always running into the Albion for free drinks, and filling up their cigarette cases with the special crested cigarettes that he had there. I was quite sure that they cost a lot of money, by the very look of them.

I deeply sympathized with him, for although we had never mentioned it, I knew that the deformed hand worried him very much, though Evelyn Shirley, who had a similar deformity, never said a word about it. I felt sorry for young Denham-Cookes, and wished that I could help him. It could have been the parson's daughter rôle in me.

As I went on waiting and wondering what all this was about, I heard the distant sound of guns again.

Recently there had been a lot of talk about a coming invasion. That did worry me. If it had come, I am sure that all of us would have died, for the most ridiculous arrangements seemed to have been made for it. Women and children would join up with wagons outside the church at Walton, which would then take them along the then very narrow road into Colchester. What nobody seemed to have recognized was that the Colchester garrison would be coming out from the city in full force to fight the battle which would be the defence of England. What would have happened to the women and children caught half way, heaven only knows. There was quite a large army stationed in Colchester at the time, and we should have lumbered along escaping the foe, only to blunder into our own men coming in the opposite direction!

I shall never know why I thought of this horror as I stood in the dining-room window, waiting for Denham to go, or for Mother to ring for me. Did I realize that I myself was standing at the crossroads of my life at this moment? On one side of me was the enemy penury, my father doing nothing, and my mother dying, and ahead of me nothing at all. I did not know what to do, for the future looked so dim, and I thought of this when standing there, and whilst I waited, the young Naval Officer whom eventually I was to marry, wrote this in his diary:

Scapa — Sea — Kirkwall.
Mouldy awful day, but we went to sea, and did some big gun firing, with 3/4 charges. As usual I didn't enjoy it much from my action station in the W/T office. Too many cyphers and codes for me to cope with all day, and tomorrow we start a proper coding staff in six watches. Calm as a pond, now. I am still carrying on with the cyphers and am still coding officer at a shilling a day. It is very hard work, and worth more than a shilling, but very interesting.

Whilst he must have been actually writing this, I was standing in the dining-room window, looking across the yard to the coach-house where dear old Mr Tricker made children's toys. He did them beautifully too. I had no idea why Mother and Arthur were so long, and wondered if by any chance he was suggesting that he married me. It was possible. The thought would please Mother enormously; it would be what she would have called 'marrying well', and she was of the era which thought a lot of that sort of thing. For my part, it would be awfully nice to have sufficient food, and no money worries, and dare to take two helpings if I felt like it!

My marriage would enchant Mother; although neither of us ever mentioned it, we both knew how dreadful it would be for me when she died. Her lease of life could not be for very long, poor darling! We tried to hide this dire secret from each other, it was the pathetic back-cloth to our existence, and it hurt all the time.

The radium treatment was holding things up, but new lumps kept appearing, and Mr Coleman did everything that he could, but instinctively all of us knew that she trod the long dark road to which there is only the one end.

Somebody had got to do something about this, I told myself, and that somebody was going to be me. I recognized it. I liked Arthur very much indeed, and was deeply sorry for him with that hand, and that ghastly old 'Ma' of his. Also I despised his fawning friends, who would accept anything he could give them, borrowed money and never repaid it, and then would go off to pastures new. What do I do next? I asked myself, and deep down in my heart somehow I *knew* what I should do. I prayed rather helplessly, turning back to the teaching that God is good and helps us. "Guide me!" I begged.

I heard the sound of the drawing-room door opening, and this was the sound that I had been waiting for, yet when I actually heard it, I thought that I was going to faint. Mother came out, through the hall, and into the dining-room.

"Arthur wants to have a word with you, dear," she said. Her tone disclosed nothing, she looked quite ordinary.

I said, again rather helplessly, "What ... what do I do?"

Then I saw that in some way she seemed to be almost her old self, with her eyes dancing, as thought she was supremely glad (she had very pretty eyes that we always used to call her 'navy-blue eyes'.) She touched me, and whispered, "This is the most wonderful thing that has ever happened to us! I ... I have been praying for it ..." and her voice broke with emotion.

I know how she must have felt. Poor poor darling!

All along I had been aware that she was terrified by the knowledge that when she died I should be left with a house full of furniture, and about £40 a year to live on. I expect she realized also that my father would offer me a home in the old rectory, but which of his women would be there with him? We never quite knew what was going on, but could guess. Possibly, when the end came, he would be surrounded by half a dozen old loves, to all of whom he had promised marriage when he was free. He was quite silly enough for that. Both of us knew that I could never have fitted into that picture. If he did offer me a home, it was not the one that I could accept.

I turned and kissed her; for a single moment we clung together (I always have the feeling that that was the actual moment when the die was cast) then I went into the drawing-room.

Arthur was standing by the empty fireplace with a great bowl of lilac in it. I remember that it was a hot day. Out of the distance yet again there came the growl of guns at sea.

"They ... they are having something of a 'do' out there." He told me a little about himself. He had a bad temper, was Irish, flew into fits of rage and broke the place up. He laughed. I must admit that I realized that this was possible. He had been brought up by a spoiling but difficult mother, and they had the most awful rows, but he had to keep in with her, because she gave him a pound a day pocket money. This complicated matters considerably. She was almost stone deaf, and never heard more than a quarter of what one said to her, which complicated everything. I agreed.

He wanted to marry me, for he had fallen in love with me the first time we had met, after that dinner party when he had sung *Little Grey Home in the West* and I had accompanied him. At that very hour, he had made up his mind that I was the girl for him.

He would give me his financial prospects; he wasn't well-off now, but when Ma died he would come into the income of £200,000, left in trust by his father. Ma had it for now. I felt that Ma could do pretty well on that! He had his army pay, about £2000 a year of his own, and the pound a day for cigarette money.

I said rather coldly "You should try living on just over £2 a week!" and then was almost ashamed of having said it.

He said, would I take £300 from him, right now, to be going on with?

"Shut up!" I told him.

He was so kind, tremendously sympathetic, and he sent the chauffeur back to the Albion to bring him three bottles of champagne to drink to the future. One for each of us, even though I did not drink. I said "But think of what it will cost!"

The house in Walton-on-the-Naze where we lived, as it is today

Myself when the war ended

and he laughed, and said that Ma would pay. I was rather stunned and not entirely ecstatic, because there were things that frightened me. I was not prepared to 'live on Ma', if he was! But Mother soothed me down. I told him that I had never liked the taste of drink, and did not want any.

"I'll soon teach you the right way to live!" and he laughed.

He never taught me. Occasionally I would have a sip to please him, no more, and from the day when he died, I have never tasted it again, save when ill, when I have had brandy.

I went upstairs to change for dinner at the Albion. I was of course one of the luckiest girls in all the world, if only because this made Mother quite another woman. She was enchanted by the whole thing. A new woman, and oh, so happy!

She saw my future suddenly secured, poor darling, and I admit that, although there was no case of my being in love with him, I did like him more than any man I had met to date, and I was intensely sorry for him. Deep down inside me, I felt that he needed help. Possibly all my training had been turning to people who wanted help, and it was part of my life.

But under it all I had the warning of premonition. I was born with this strange psychic ability: I know when trouble is coming. I read between the lines in the book of life, and this is not a happy thing.

I told him that I was not in love, in the accepted sense, that I was deeply fond of him, and would do anything that I could to make him happy. He laughed and said that there was no worry about not being sufficiently in love, for he had buckets full of it, quite enough for both of us.

But all through the talk I did realize that he was terrified of his mother, who apparently kept on and on threatening to stop this allowance which she paid him. He was wildly extravagant, and knew it. There seemed to be no likelihood of his changing, and I was right there.

His father had originally married an heiress, when he was twenty-two, and had had five daughters, all but one of them dying. The one was Lady Arthur Hill, who wrote *In the Gloaming, O my Darling*. I attributed Arthur's strong musical sense to that side of the family, and he adored music. The old Colonel had died when Arthur was five years old, and he could only faintly remember him.

I knew from that talk that Mrs Denham-Cookes was going to be a difficult woman, and one of our officers later told me that he had met her. He had gone to a party for the troops, held in the gorgeous drawing-room at number 6 Prince's Gate, and he said that she was "mad as a hatter, only a bit more so!" Then he had gone on to say "And as to that awful sister of his ...!" but I cut him short. Later, of course, I was to find how right he had been, but I could not stand by and listen to that sort of story. If I was going to marry into the family, I could not stand by and hear my future in-laws run down. It was all extremely difficult for we had no money, and the thought of a trousseau was a nightmare. I sold some of the little 'pieces' one collects as a girl, not at vast profit, for I always find things lose in value and do not come up in value ever, leastways not for me.

Then it was a very difficult time, and all the while Mother's condition was worsening, and it really was terribly worrying and difficult. Mrs Denham-Cookes would not come to the wedding, which infuriated her son, of course, and I admit it was disappointing for him, but she was this sort of woman. I felt sure that trouble lay ahead with her.

My husband-to-be was settling money on me, and apparently with a marriage settlement, the father of the bride does the same. I felt sure that this was going to be difficult, but my father *had* some money left him by his mother, and he came down to see us about all this.

I had a straight talk with my father and told him that he had done very little to make my position in this life more secure, to which his reply was "You could always have come home, you know."

But how could we have done that?

It was wonderful the effect that my engagement had on my mother, who was enchanted by it. She was very fond of Arthur; they got on so well together, and her complete happiness silenced any doubts that there might have been in me. Now, what was the next move?

The first thing to do was for us to go up to London and have tea with Mrs Denham-Cookes at number 6 Prince's Gate. After the Second World War, it became the German Embassy (she would not have liked that one, I am sure.) Once I had to go there for some information I wanted to get about the girl Eva Broun. I told the German who interviewed me that once this had been my husband's house, and he said, "This is indeed the most beautiful room!" (I hardly dared confess that it had been the cook's bedroom!)

Going to visit my future mother-in-law, meant some new clothes, and hardly the sort that one made oneself. Mother and I went over to Colchester, and she bought a navy blue suit for me, with a pale pink blouse and matching hat. I was most deeply indebted to her for it.

But how brave of her when she was so ill, to attempt the extremely tiring day trip to London, and back! Her condition was now worsening all the time, and there were moments when she looked desperately ill. But the comfort was that a great load of anxiety had been lifted from her shoulders, and she was so happy about everything that the whole idea had given her new strength.

I do admit that when we found ourselves standing on the handsome step of 6 Prince's Gate, I had a most ghastly apprehension. It was dreadful meeting a stone deaf mother-in-law for the first time, even worse when you knew already what a difficult woman she could be.

Chown, the butler, opened the door, and behind him lay a huge sprawling hall, with a beautiful red-carpeted stairway rising at the far end. Arthur had told me that Chown had been the butler there when he himself had been born, and instinctively I recognized him as being a friend. This he always was to me, bless him.

"Mrs Denham-Cookes?" Mother asked, and with confidence.

He made the horrifying statement "Mrs Denham-Cookes is not receiving this afternoon."

I simply could *not* believe it.

She knew, of course, how ill Mother was, for Arthur had told her, and at that moment I felt as if part of me had turned to ice. It had been such a desperate effort for my poor mother to make, because she was far too ill at the time to come, but had done this for my sake. Let alone the money we had had to spend on the fares, getting new clothes for it. Even a little food at a restaurant (a cheap one, of course), but we had had to have something. It meant less food for the rest of the week, as we both knew.

Rather vaguely my mother said, "But she was expecting us."

Again, in true butler manner, Chown repeated the unhappy statement that Mrs Denham-Cookes was not receiving this afternoon!

Years later when Chown got to know me very well he confessed how indignant he had been about the whole affair. He had thought that it was utterly disgraceful, but that was the message that he had been told to deliver, and there was nothing else that he could do about it. Unhappily there was nothing more that Mother or I could do, but say "Good afternoon," and turn away from the hateful house.

When we finally got back to Liverpool Street to take the train home again, Mother was half-collapsed, and ultimately when we got back to Walton (to be met by Arthur, with the chauffeur and the car) she could hardly speak from sheer exhaustion. It was I who told him what had happened (and in no measured terms either, for I was furiously angry). I did not care if the chauffeur was listening, he probably knew already the sort of woman that she was, and if he hadn't known before, most certainly he knew right now!

At that moment I came closer to breaking off the engagement than at any other time, and would have done it without a second thought, for I was indignant. Arthur flew right off the handle, I don't think that I have ever seen a man so angry. He then announced that he would load up a revolver, drive to London, and shoot his mother! This was hardly the retaliation that I had anticipated, and I was surprised, to say the least of it.

"You can't possibly do that," I said, "There ... there may have been some muddle ..." I was beginning to make excuses for her. He seemed to be so terribly angry that he alarmed me.

"She is going to learn her lesson," said he, and he had gone quite white with sheer anger.

Possibly my main anxiety was for my mother, who had made

this tremendous effort, and now was feeling a bad reaction from it. Both of us felt sure that the marriage would never be, and I knew how much this would worry her. We got her home, and to bed, it was the only thing to do. I tried to reassure her, and when she was a little better, I rang up the Albion Hotel, only to find that Arthur had already started for London, and would be at Colchester by now. For the first time I was really frightened that he would do something foolish but there was absolutely nothing that I could do.

I rang off and tried not to think of it. Would he really shoot his mother? Surely not! How could he even think of anything like that? Or had he just said it in anger? He always said that he had a frightful temper, and it rather looked as if it was almost more than that. I walked back home from the 'phone box, and I thought that a temper of that kind would be hard to live with, but he had, of course, been provoked. I did not think that he would actually shoot her, but again I did not know quite what to think. I began to wish that I was out of the whole affair.

Next day after lunch, when Mother was having her lie-down, Arthur walked in. Most certainly he had gone to London and had stalked into his mother's room at ten o'clock that night, revolver and all! His mother had said that it had been a ghastly mistake, and that Chown had misunderstood her directions. I don't suppose that Arthur quite believed that, for Chown was always most reliable, but in the end his mother had given him a fat cheque, £100, which I thought an unbelievable miracle, and which he said was "nothing like enough, seeing the damned silly mess she had made of everything for him". He also brought back with him a letter; he said it was a letter of apology, but I never found anything of that in it. It was speaking of a mistake having been made, and written in the most dreadful handwriting, which was almost impossible to read.

She hoped to see me as soon as a meeting could be arranged, so she said. I don't suppose she "hoped it" for a single moment, but could say nothing else.

He himself took me up to London to see her, a week later, for Mother was still too exhausted, and could not do it.

The house was glorious, of course, with a dining-room that

could seat thirty, and an austere library behind it where we met. How deaf that poor woman was! No wonder that she got hold of the wrong ideas, for you never knew if she had heard you or not.

Once she must have been radiantly beautiful (she was still very pretty) but was extremely bigoted, and I could not like her. At this time she was giving enormous tea-parties to the troops, held in the drawing-room (big enough to use as a ballroom if you felt like it). Kitty, who would be my sister-in-law, got up and sang *Oh, for a night in Bohemia* to the troops, who must have been bored stiff. Kitty was *nobody's* idea of a night in Bohemia!

I met 'Jim', who had been Arthur's old nannie, but there seemed to be a dense curtain between us all the time. I was not one of them (thank God!), and they were treating me like a fairly superior servant! All save Chown, who was quite wonderful. Arthur was obviously scared stiff of his mother and dared not say 'no' to her_ his mind for ever on the pound a day pocket money, which she was ever threatening to stop.

We were to be married in Frinton, for the regiment had been moved there, and the C.O. wished this. It would be in November, in the little old church which was so sweet. Mrs Denham-Cookes told me she would send me all the linen. I said that I had a good deal, for my Uncle Herbert (my father's brother) was 'in' linen in Belfast, and every Christmas had brought Mother a load. She said that here would be a very different sort from the ones my uncle had given us. It *was*! It was utterly shoddy compared to his.

This would be a simple wedding, and she wished this. We should only get three days' leave for the honeymoon, and she insisted that we went to Bournemouth, which was the proper place to go now that the south of France was cut off.

Returning to Walton, I felt that it had gone wrong! She and I meant nothing to each other, and I was well aware that she disliked me. But I had liked her brother, Lord Lurgan, who came in to see me, and said, "Don't pay any attention to Clar, she talks a lot of nonsense!" which was the way *he* felt about it!

At the R.A.C. I met Arthur's grandmother, old Lady Lurgan, who was a *pet*! She was a woman entirely after my own heart, and she said of her daughter who was to be my mother-in-law, "Clar makes me sick. I know she can't hear a word, but she does not even try to listen, and she always *was* like that."

How true it was!

Mother was thankful that the meeting had passed off all right, and also enormously relieved. I did not tell her that I thought the old lady was a bit mad really, and, as far as I could see, so did the rest of her family. Apparently she had been spoilt as a child, because of her deafness, and in her thirties when she had given up all hope of marriage, my very wealthy father-in-law had married her. Anyway the awful interview was behind me, and now we settled down to preparing for the November wedding in Frinton church.

7

A SEA OF TROUBLES

During my engagement I was not entirely happy about everything. A dreadful feeling of premonition hung over me. It was hard to cope with this, for there was no reason to be afraid, and I attributed it to the fact that possibly every girl felt the same approaching her marriage.

Mother and I made the trousseau, being both good needlewomen. There was one ghastly moment when that eternal butter-in Mrs Denham-Cookes sent me word by her son that she disapproved of my parents having split, and suggested that we went back to Whitchurch for the wedding! She disapproved of broken marriages, and thought this would be a good idea.

I rose then, and I think I petrified Denham for I was in a wild temper! The separation of my parents had nothing to do with Mrs Denham-Cookes, and she *must* mind her own business! Arthur was horrified! He very seldom stood up against his mother, but he did this time. It was then that I found he was terrified of her dropping his pound a day pocket-money, but with his £2000 a year and his pay behind that, I should have thought it was a mere flea-bite, and said so.

I asked "Why is it that you want so much money? People can live on very little, you know."

He went rather white, and when he paled he always gave the appearance of being most dreadfully ill. He apologized, and after a bit he said that he was one of those men who was used to spending money fairly freely, and he always had done so. But anyway he went up to London in the car, and he saw his mother, and we had no further trouble with her after that.

The wedding invitations were sent out, and immediately the

most marvellous gifts started to arrive. Mother was wildly interested in every parcel as it came. They really were quite wonderful.

But there was one strange incident which I found most disconcerting.

It took place three weeks before the wedding, one of those days when the gunfire had been particularly noisy at Walton. Mother lay down every afternoon, so I hoped she was asleep when a friend of ours, a rather older captain, and a widower, came round. In civilian life he was a solicitor, with a little boy of seven years old, whom I had had to tea, and had played with him several times. The captain had originally come in for a sing-song, but I did not know him very well, and was surprised to see him on the step.

"Oh, do come in," I said.

He came in, sat down, and after a short while told me why he had come. It was disquieting.

He hedged for a bit, and then he came to the point. Was I quite sure that it was a wise thing to do to marry Mr Denham-Cookes? I did not know what to say, because I was so surprised. He looked really worried, and said that he hoped I would understand he was speaking for my own good, but he very much wished that I would think about it again. By now I was extremely worried because obviously he was in earnest. Arthur was gay and a quite delightful young man; I was happy with him, and said so. I knew that his mother was dreadful, but that was hardly his fault, and mercifully she was an imaginary invalid and stayed in Prince's Gate, so that I should not see too much of her.

He was very quiet, and his whole manner was most convincing. He said that he had come to warn me because he thought this to be his duty, and he was very worried about it. In fact he would rather marry me himself than let this happen! (Now we *are* coming down to facts, I told myself.)

I did try to find out what it was he meant by warning me like this; was Arthur already married, and I did not know it? This amused him. He said, "Of course not!" In the end I got rid of him, but it was a most irksome meeting, and I did not tell Mother anything about it lest it upset her.

Three months later, I knew exactly what he had meant and admired the courage which had brought him to the house. By then he had been killed in France. He had made a very brave attempt to help me.

Ten days later, I was married to Arthur, on one of those half-foggy November days which drift in from the sea in that part of the world, and all day long there was the far sound of guns growling.

What was Robbie doing then?

He was in luck, for he had been sent out to Hong Kong to serve there for three years, right out of the war, and I think he was having the time of his life! He fell in love with China, and everyone whom he met, and was determined to learn Chinese, which he did. Later, when he returned to England, he passed an exam in it, when he had to put the *Daily Mail* leading article into Chinese, of all awful things!

For a quiet, home-loving young man, brought up with few friends (for his family were the very opposite of mine in that way) Hong Kong must have been a miraculous change for him.

He wrote:

14th Nov. 1916. Hong Kong.
For once in a way I was quite busy all day. We went ashore at 4.15, and played tennis at the club. After dinner played Pin Pool at the Dockyard Club.

He was living in a different world, one which the war did not touch, though he had not been there many days before he got the news that his only brother Gerald had been killed at the front. At Walton the guns were noisy at sea, and the fog was creeping inland. What next?

The night before my wedding Mother gave a party at the Marine Hotel. I was worried about this expense, and in the afternoon, without her knowing, I slipped out into the little street, with my silver hairbrushes and the knick-knacks which had seen me through my girlhood. I took the proceeds round to the Marine Hotel, and saw the owner old Mr Barker there, who was very nice. I told him that Mother would come for the bill tomorrow, and I wanted him to tell her there wasn't one. He seemed surprised, then he took the money and said "Thank you", then "What a very kind person you must be!" It was then that I realized that he knew how hard-up we had always been.

That night Mother and I walked round to the hotel together, and somehow that seemed to be the last time that we were ever together in quite the same way. Possibly that was the hour when we parted. After that too much happened, there was too much to do, and later on I was to find myself too hopelessly lost in the fantastic new world to which I belonged, and far too troubled.

I remember walking hand-in-hand, and the smell of the tamarisk hedge which I always liked so much. I remember I said "I love you so, I just love you ..."

Whatever happened, I must not cry, but this *was* goodbye. She hated parting with me, but she felt that the marriage made me secure, and she would not be leaving me alone as she had dreaded.

That very week all our arrangements for the future had been changed because of his mother again. We were to have gone on living in rooms as he was doing now with Mrs Edwards whom I liked. His mother said that we had got to get a furnished house, and as he dare not disobey her for a moment, I had had to rush over to Frinton to get one. There were dozens to choose from, for the people had fled from the dangerous east coast. I took Thalassa, next door to the Queen's Hotel, with ten bedrooms, and believe it or not I got it for £2 a week! Apparently it was about to be billeted, and the owners would let it go for anything to save it from that. It had been owned by the editor of the *Boys' Own Paper*, which I had always adored, and I recognized some of the pictures on the walls.

I got staff easily: Mrs Fanthorpe from Walton to be cook, Hatcher, a nice girl as parlour maid, and Jackson as a tweeny. Jenner who had been with Arthur at Cambridge, would be butler-batman, and there was his own batman as well. Jenner was a completely silent man! I have always wondered how he felt about the whole thing, for I never knew. He was for some months in the background of my life, and the day he left, he walked out for ever. I have often wondered what happened to him.

The wedding went off well. My father arrived for it, and a

dreadful aunt of mine from Ashford. You could only get into the church by ticket. Denham's car fetched me, for I could not drive with Dad (that was too much for anyone). He was to meet me at the church porch. I took my own lady's maid, her mother had worked for us when we lived at St Albans, and she had always wanted a young mistress.

It seems frightful, but at that moment I did not think I could bear the drive with my father: it would be too much. He was waiting for me, far more nervous than I was. The church was packed, and it took three clergy to marry us. I can never think why. As we left the church and came through the guard of honour, a young soldier burst out of the crowd. It happened to be Arthur's cousin, the younger Rowley boy, Sir Joshua's son, gay, excited and very interested. He was killed three weeks later.

I hated the reception at Beach House, though everybody was most kind. I left wearing the fur coat (my first one) that somehow or other Mother had managed to give me — I shall never know how.

As Arthur's mother had directed, we shot down to Bournemouth for one hateful night, returning to lunch in London with Lord Lurgan, who had all the family to meet me. Uncle Billy was a darling (the best of that bunch, I always felt.) His advice to me about my mother-in-law was "Don't pay any attention to a single thing that Clar says! She never knows what she's talking about"!

When I returned to Frinton again, only three days had passed by, but the whole of my world seemed to have changed. Mother had put the furniture into store helped by my aunt, who I gathered had been most difficult. She had come to live in what was then a boarding-house (The Cecil, today it is a hotel) further along the front. I had very much wanted her to be with us. We had ten bedrooms, and all the staff on the top floor, so there was lots of room. But apparently Denham's mother had warned him against this one, so he had to say 'no', and nothing would change him.

I did find Arthur very odd about money. He gave me a most meagre housekeeping allowance, even for someone well accustomed to economizing as I was. I could have nothing for myself. No dress allowance, no pocket money! He would always give me something when I asked for it, but only the exact sum. That wretched Ma of his had again warned him, that "if I had the money I might run away", and he stuck to this to his dying day!

About everything I had an awful apprehension. The house was running well, but somewhere something was all wrong, and I knew this. I became aware in a vague way of my own of ruffled agitation within myself, which acted as a warning. There was something about all this, that I did not understand.

Arthur was a charmer, but at times he could be most remote, and very liable to fly into the sort of temper that had never been allowed at the rectory. Spontaneously amusing, he could on the contrary be deeply moody, as though he held possession of some secret which nobody could share with him. I told myself that although the Irish can be so delightfully charming, they can be the complete opposite. He corroborated this.

"I'm Irish," he said, "and if that doesn't explain everything, begorra, what does?"

I knew that he had always slept badly, whereas I just dropped off the moment I put my head on a pillow. He apparently wandered round the house half the night, for, if I woke, he was never there. It worried me when he went on early parade after so little sleep.

He wanted people to dinner most nights, for he loved a crowd, but he did expect me to cater for visitors, four servants, a butler and a batman, on £7 a week, which was almost impossible. Food was still fairly cheap, and the cook's father did the most excellent poaching on Walton backwater (at the most reasonable cost) but Denham *was* asking too much.

Under it all I was depressed. Mother was wildly happy about everything, but she was getting so much worse all the time, and this was heart-breaking. The trouble about Arthur behaving oddly at times (up most of the night, and always spending too much money) was one that I had to learn to live with. In a muddle, he always wrote to Ma, which I thought was wrong. I worried but could do nothing. Perhaps I was just feeling my way.

One very early morning, when it was still dark, the guns at sea had been so noisy that they woke me; it would be about four o'clock, and I could not get to sleep again. Arthur was absent, and when he did not return I became a little alarmed, and went out trying to find where he was. I put on a kimono and some slippers, and when I got on to the landing I heard a faint sound in Arthur's dressing-room alongside. I went into it. He was sitting in the armchair, leaning forward with his head dropped into his hands, and crying like a girl! By his side was about a quarter of a bottle of whisky, and the whole place reeked of it.

That was the moment when I KNEW.

He wept bitterly. I shall never forget how pitifully the poor thing sobbed, and then he confessed that he simply could not live without drink. I said, "I'll help. You've got *me* now!" and tried to comfort him. My father could cry when he was in a real mess with one of his women, but I have never seen anything quite as terrible as this poor young man's tears! He was at the end of his tether. He confessed that he simply could not face the world without the courage that whisky gave him, and it had been so for years. He was twenty-four, and all his life he had fallen back on spirits to see him through. It had begun in France, when his mother would not let him drink the water without spirits in it, "to make it safe", so she thought.

I got him back to bed, comforting him, and when he was a little quieter, slipped back into the dressing-room to tidy it up, so that Jenner would not notice anything when he came along. But of course Jenner must have known, for he had been at Trinity Hall with Arthur, and this had been going on for years.

He begged me never to leave him, a thought which had never entered my head. It was the last thing that I should have done and I said so, reminding him that marriage was until death.

It had all began when he found that drink eased his shyness. I blamed his mother. I had disliked her from the first, when Mother and I had been turned from the door, after making all that journey. Beautiful as she was, I could not bring myself to like her. She had told him that it was "vulgar" not to drink, and even Chown had been astounded that anyone with the name of Denham-Cookes could ask for common-to-God water!

I suppose the poor man had always been ashamed of, and worried by that malformed hand of his. Then, when he had been nine years old, he nearly died with pneumonia, which barred him from going to school and mixing with others, which I am sure would have helped him enormously at that time. But Mrs Denham-Cookes, backed by her doctors, said "no".

If only his mother had died instead of his father, I believe that he could have been alive today, and none of this need have happened. He hated isolation, which she encouraged, and loved mixing with others, something that she prevented.

Of course when he got loose, and went to Trinity Hall, it was the first time in his life when he actually got away from Ma, and *how* he loved it! He had been coached for this, by several members of the Galer family, who lived in Dulwich, with five sons who supplemented rather meagre means by coaching. Between them they got him into Cambridge, and here for the first time in his life he got away from Ma. She could no longer lay down the law, save by letter and although she was eternally threatening to stop his allowance, she had to pay his bills. I should think that they were enormous, for he was a wild spendthrift.

At Cambridge he got a car, a chauffeur, a dog and he had fun. There he had met Rogers-Tillstone, the man to whom I was to owe so much later on.

I can say with truth that I believe Arthur had never been drunk in the accepted sense, because he was one of those men whom it had never affected that way though I am sure also that after breakfast he was never absolutely sober. The whole thing was a tragic story, and, whatever happened, Mother must *not* know about this.

I shall never forget the horror of that morning when we talked in his dressing-room, and later when I tried to hide the traces of what had been going on from his valet. I said that I would find a doctor to help him. The thing was not incurable. He had believed that, if I found out, I should leave him immediately, and I must say that he did not know me very well. By the time that his valet and my maid appeared nobody would have had any clue that something had happened during the night.

My son, Pip, aged 8

With my second husband Robbie, Commander C. G. Robinson, R.N.

What I wanted was a specialist in this sort of thing, and not one of his mother's choosing! It was no good going to one of the local men, lest the talk got around, and this was highly secret. He had to be guarded, and I was the right woman for this.

The next thing that happened was a surprise. I had written to the authorities about Mother's condition and saying that she could not live, and could we get Joscelyn – who was in Egypt – back for at least a fortnight? I never thought that it would work, but one morning early and quite unexpectedly he walked into the house.

Apparently he had got to Frinton by the last train the previous night, and had had a shake-down with one of Arthur's men, (which did not go down too well) and came along early to Thalassa. At this time old General Stevens was staying with us, and my brother was a lance-corporal! It was unthinkable for a lance-corporal to sit at the same table as a general, even in a private house. I must say I was having a lot to trouble me, and life was getting a bit too difficult.

The minute we had finished breakfast I rushed out round to Mr Loose's shop (always my sheet-anchor in times of trouble), and bought my brother a plain clothes suit, with the result that every time he went out he was pestered by awful women with white feathers. It really was the most awkward situation. This visit was terribly hard to stage-manage. It would mean a second parting for him from Mother, and I did not know how she would take it. I tried to persuade the General to help me get a commission for Joscelyn. Then he would be able to stay in England for training for a few months, and he could be with Mother. She had been so enchanted to see him, that I felt something more must be done. The General helped. But, of course, Joscelyn had never been very good at interviews, and always gave the wrong impression of himself. He went up to London, and was interviewed, but it did not work out. It would have been better if he had gone to a more established school, I am sure, but our bother all through had always been no money, and I thought that he had been jolly lucky going to school at all.

In the end, he had to return to Egypt with that awful journey out (mines everywhere, as we all knew). He would be fairly safe when he got there (anything was better than going to France), but it was the getting there that caused the trouble, for undoubtedly the high seas were dangerous.

After he had gone (I had left him and Mother to make their farewells alone together) I went round to the Cecil to see her. She was lower than I had ever seen her before, for, of course both of us knew that she would never see him again. It was a very dreadful feeling. I dared not tell her how anxious I was about my own marriage, for again there had been trouble with Arthur. He was a captain now. At all costs I could not worry her about him.

I did not know how to comfort Mother. I took her home to dine with us, but she was in a sorry condition, and I had the dreadful idea that perhaps parting with Joscelyn for ever, could be the last straw.

At this time Arthur must have said something to his mother because we went to London for the night, staying at Berners Hotel, and he talked to her for four hours. He was in debt, I think, and wanting more money, which he got. When I returned home, she wrote me the most dreadful letter, saying that I must try not to influence my husband so much, for he knew what to do, and I did not, having been brought up in that wretched country rectory. It was infuriating. What I wanted was a good doctor to help him, nothing more, and I seemed to be helpless.

It was more worrying because it was plain that Mother was very much worse. I had three spare bedrooms and wanted to get her into the house with a nurse, but Arthur would have none of it. I think that privately he was afraid of cancer, and thought that it was infectious.

I could not turn to my father, for it seemed that he had been extremely angry about my Christmas present to him. The truth was that Arthur would not give me any money for Christmas presents even though I asked for it; he would not even give me 'pin money'. Because of this, I had been able to send my father for Christmas only three pairs of socks, for which he never thanked me. They took every shilling that I had got. The result was that I did not get even a Christmas card from him.

I remember a bleak January day at the turn of the year, which can be quite merciless in that part of the world. I went down to the deserted beach, and sat there on a seat, to have a really good cry! It is a woman's refuge in times of real pain. What must my poor mother think of me? She was dying now, I knew, perhaps not immediately, but it could not be very far away, and there was absolutely nothing that I could do. My father would not speak to me, and nowhere could I find the help that my husband needed so much. I just sobbed my heart out. I remember the biting cold of that afternoon, with the sun falling and the far-off sound of guns (we never seemed to get out of that echo), I prayed. It is so dreadful when prayer is not answered.

Out in Hong King, the man whom I would eventually marry, was basking in glorious sunshine, with no hint of a war being on. He wrote in his diary:

Hong Kong. 16th Feb. Thursday.
Wright and I went ashore after tiffin and went to a stamp shop, where we went halves on a 6d packet of 1,000 stamps. We spent the afternoon in sorting them out, having to work in the evening to make up for it. The Commodore has got a mania for economy at present, and he wants everybody to send home a monthly subscription to some war charity! Nothing doing!

How easy life must have been for him, far from the war, and from home, it is true, but if a man joins the Royal Navy he does so, knowing that it is not the life for a home bird, surely? At this moment when he was gaily buying stamps in glorious sunshine, I was crying my heart out on the deserted beach at Frinton. "Oh God", I prayed, "what do I *do*?"

I felt strangely ill, and no wonder, so I went to see one of the very few friends that I had. He was an army doctor, who at the time was stationed in Thorpe-le-Soken. He was an understanding man, and I realized that he knew without my telling him the conditions under which I was living.

He said that I was pregnant. Talk about the last straw!

He was quite plain-spoken and ready to advise me as to what to do. He did not think that poor Mother would last very long (that in itself was an agony) and he suggested that I got medical aid for Arthur. He gave me something to make me better (which worked) and I was to go back in a fortnight which I did, only to find that suddenly he had been posted to France and had gone.

I had the vague idea that my last hope had gone with him!

Mother was feeling so ill that I found a small nursing-home in St Mary's Road for her, and I went round there to see the nurse in charge. They happened to have a free room, and she would be better there than in digs, so I arranged for her to move in right away. Anyway she would get some care, which she was not getting now.

The nurse was quite nice, but these people who work with death so continually become accustomed to it, so that they never can help you in quite the same way. When I told Mother about it, she conformed to the idea, and I packed her things, and the nurse fetched her in a cab that afternoon. I was late home for lunch as a result of this.

"Where the hell have *you* been?" asked Arthur in front of the butler, who discreetly left the room.

He came down to hard facts, and they *were* hard. I knew, of course, that because he was worried he had been drinking more heavily, poor thing, and only hoped that nobody else knew about it. Now trouble had come with the C.O. Arthur had been called in to see him. He hesitated at first, then he told me how miserably uneasy he was, for he thought that he was going to lose a 'pip'. For a moment I did not realize what this meant, then my eye went to the pips on his cuff. Surely ... having got it ... surely they couldn't take it away again? Scarcely knowing what I was saying, I asked him "Why?"

He flew into the most violent temper.

Apparently he had been relieved of duty while things were hanging in the balance, and this alone was a very bad sign, or so it seemed to me. A horrible whispering sort of nervousness appeared to be going on inside me, like a murmur that I could not control. I did not know what to do. He had made all the arrangements to go up to London to save his pip. Lord Lurgan would help him; his mother would get influence to bear; but at all costs he had got to see them, and as soon as possible. I made the foolish remark that I thought Conky (pet name for Colonel Concannon) was possibly able to run his own regiment without outside interference and might strongly object if it were called in. The moment this family got into any trouble, it seemed that they called up a few titles, to administer what was known in the family as being "a little push". But I could not see this working, if Conky was angry, he would stay angry, and surely nobody could make him stop, depriving Denham of a pip, if he thought it was the *right* thing to do? I said that Mother was worse; I wanted to stay here in Frinton with her.

He was abrupt.

"You are coming with me," he said.

I told him what I had done about Mother, and I went up to see her that afternoon, not liking at all the fact that I had got to break the ghastly news to her, that I was going to London with Arthur next day. She felt better. She said that she had had a lovely lunch, but the home wanted her to have a night nurse. I arranged this. I rang up the doctor. He was Dr Craigie Bell, a man whom all the Frintonian women adored, and I could never think why. He was one of the jolly kind! He reassured me that Mother was in no danger of dying, she had had a really bad cold, which had pulled her down but she would be herself again within the week. It was my pregnancy that made me nervous. The thing to do was to go up to London, for I should return to find her lots better.

I relied on this.

She seemed happy that afternoon, but her voice was very faint and tired. After dinner that night, Arthur and I went round to see her again. She seemed better, but her voice was not her own, and I said so. As we were leaving, she said to me "I do wish you would take little Juliet with you." I remember going back into the bedroom and scooping the dog up into my arms. She looked at me, and she said "Do kiss me again."

There are some moments in life that one never forgets, and this was one of them. She did not want me to go to London, and heaven only knows how much I hated leaving her, but what could I do? I was living through an almost unendurable anguish, and I am today afraid that she was sharing some of it. I pray not. I dared not stay.

The nurse came to Thalassa at six the next morning, when it was very dark, and a dense fog was hanging over the sea.

Mother had died at four o'clock in the morning.

I did not cry.

I got up and dressed, hardly knowing what I was doing, divided between a tearing self-reproach and the remembrance that we had to get up to London this morning to try to save that pip. Dear Mr Knight the clergyman came down to see me. I was very grateful to see a clergyman, someone like what Dad could be in his better mood, someone affectionate and wanting to help. I am sure that he knew far better than I realized at the time, how dreadful my position was, for he was so gentle. I sent my father a telegram and got no reply. Years later, I found in his diary these words:

> My wife died this morning. I went to tea with Scarlett Potter, and saw some most interesting seals.

We started off to London early, for Arthur was impatient. I remember that we had to change at Colchester, with a twenty-minute wait, which seemed like an eternity. He left me sitting on a seat, whilst he went to get a drink. A kind old lady spoke to me, asking, "Are you all right, dear?" and I said that I was.

I blamed myself for not having stayed with Mother last night, but what could I have done? The doctor told me she was perfectly all right. Apparently her heart had failed. Maybe it was the kind way out. Nothing could have helped her. How unfair God is, I thought, how grossly unfair!

When we got to London the car met us, and we went straight to Berners Hotel, where we always stayed; he left me in the bedroom there, whilst he went along to Prince's Gate to see Ma. I could not see for the life of me what Ma could do to solve that wretched pip. When he did return, undoubtedly she had stemmed the worry with false courage, and he had got Hugh Galer, who was a solicitor and had been his best man, with him.

I knew little more about it, save that I lay for hours on that bed, whilst Hugh and Arthur went the rounds, trying to do something clever, and using every possible bit of influence that they had got. I never thought that it would be sufficient, but what could I do to help?. I recall little of the rest of it, only a sense of collapse and hopeless despair. Two days later I was unpicking the third pip from his uniform cuff.

I did not go to Mother's funeral because I could not have borne
it, and I had the coming baby to think of. I knew that by now
Joscelyn would have got my cable and I wired again to my
father, telling him when the funeral would be, and once more
there was no reply. She was to be buried in the tiny churchyard
of one of the smallest churches in England, the one where we had
been married. I was dazed by grief, for I had never expected this
so suddenly, and I was worried that it could affect the baby. And
what would happen to Arthur now.

Within the week, he was moved from Frinton itself to what
was know as Holland Camp at Holland Gat, halfway to
Clacton-on-Sea. Here the water comes in deeply, which had all
along made it a suspicious point for suitable invasion. It was a
lonely camp: a few wooden huts, and mostly tents, bitterly cold
at this time of the year, and, believe me, the east coast has the
most diabolical early springtime.

I of course was left alone with the servants at Thalassa, but
apparently the coming baby had survived all the trouble, and this
was something.

My father had never got in touch with me; he had not even
written! He must have always known how much Mother meant
to me, and the fact that I was so utterly alone hurt me most
dreadfully. I felt that he should have helped. It was then that I
received a long letter from one of the women in the village, most
sympathetically understanding, and so kind. She knew how I
would feel, had been fond of Mother, and realized that we had
meant a great deal to each other.

My father's banns had been read out the next Sunday, and he
was going to marry Miss Sims after the third reading. I am
ashamed to say that I saw red.

Perhaps there is some truth in the rumour of the last straw
breaking the camel's back, and indeed, when you came to think
of it, I *had* been something of a camel, bearing all the big burdens
of my father's bad behaviour! He had never written nor had he
come to the funeral, now he was just going to marry again, the
first moment that he was free.

I should never have acted as I did. But all along I had felt that
the Bishop had been far too nice to him, and I do think that he

should have warned Dad that if his bad behaviour continued, then he would have to take action. I told the Bishop exactly what had happened.

He wrote back regretting the source from which the information had come, and he told me that now my father would cease to be a priest. There was no fuss, no unfrocking or anything of that kind, but he was no longer a parson.

He married Josephine Sims three weeks afterwards, and, poor man, how much he was to regret it later on!

I must say that I was more than deeply shocked at the way he had rushed his second marriage, completely ignoring me when he must have known how tragically upset I was. I believe that he was under great pressure, with no idea of my own circumstances and the complications of my new life.

He had to leave Whitchurch, but he was married in the little church by his friend Mr Morgan who had taken Mr Thrupp's place at Alderminster. I wondered if any of these men thought about Mother and myself and what we had been through. I doubt it. He then came to London to work, carrying on with pedigrees, the translation and cataloguing of old deeds, and was well known at the Record Office. We were not to meet again for some time. I wished that I had never taken the action that I did take, for he could be such an enchanting man, and so brilliantly clever. If only he had not been so ridiculously love-sick!

Now Arthur was stationed at the camp at Holland Gat, one of the most dangerous places along the coast, it was felt, and then suddenly he was moved right away to Falmouth! I had found it difficult to visit him at the camp, and it was all wrong to have him staying on with men who knew him, and he one pip down. His men adored him, this is no biased opinion, but it was most marked from time to time.

He went on ahead down to Falmouth to get a furnished house for us there; this, we were told, should be fairly easy, and I was left behind to close down Thalassa, which I loved. Today it has been pulled down, and some quite horrible-looking flats have taken its place and that of Yarra, the house once next door to Thalassa. Frinton has lost its old beauty of atmosphere, when it was so well kept and quite charming. Today it is just another seaside place, no more.

I had got all Mother's furniture from Hertford House in store, which was a worry, and I felt that I had to do something about this, so I took a small house (ridiculously called Poona) in the Harold Road, so we were away from the front and did not have to have double glass windows, and this would take the furniture until we made another move. If Arthur had to go to the front, which God forbid, then it would be my home.

Now Arthur was attached to the Rifle Brigade, which angered him very much, for he had started the war in the Irish Guards, and what he said about the Rifle Brigade was quite unprintable.

Mercifully by this time I had met Stanley Nicholson, a solicitor living in Walton, for he had drawn up Mother's will for her. He came to see me about this, when I was really in trouble, because Arthur had left me with a cheque for £100 to pay everything up and get myself and the servants down to Falmouth, and the first bill that had come in was from the Off Licence of the Queen's Hotel, for £97! Even *my* arithmetic was disturbed by it! I had to get myself, Fanthorpe, Jackson and the maids, all down to Falmouth (and Juliet the dog – nothing would make me part with her) and I did not know what to do. Also I feared that if this one most horrifying bill could arrive, there might be others pursuing me! Mr Nicholson was most kind and helpful. He took over for me, and somehow he did not seem to be at all surprised that this had happened. He said that there was no need for concern. He would settle it.

The maids started at dawn, and I and Juliet followed by the nine o'clock train. In London we crossed to Paddington, and there we started off on that almost eternal journey on which I really did think that I should die.

Arthur had rung me up two nights previously, to say that he had taken a terraced house, in the artists' quarter, which was quiet, and overlooked a lovely park. The place was very full, for people had gone down there to escape the war and as far as he could see, nobody knew that there was a war on! We left Frinton at nine, and arrived at Falmouth at five minutes to midnight. At one time I thought the baby would be born in the train. When I got into the waiting car I burst into tears from sheer exhaustion! I remember that the terraced house was sweetly pretty, and covered with small white roses which smelt delicious.

Fanthorpe and Jackson were installed, but I was too tired to bother about food. I went straight to bed.

I was awakened early next day by reveille, for the camp was almost alongside us. At ten-thirty, a car appeared, and the man told me that Arthur had ordered it to come every day, and take me down into the town shopping, and bring me back. I was horrified at the expense of all this! He really *was* the most extravagant man. I took it that day, but I told him that the next day I'd walk down.

It was during lunch that I had to confess to that shocking wine bill which had come in, and put me the wrong side of the count! Arthur was furious about it. It was nothing to do with him, of course! It was a dirty lie, a try-on, said he. He owed nothing like that, and the Queen's Hotel had been out for a diddle! He blamed Stanley Nicholson for paying it, he himself would have preferred to be sued for it, because he could prove that it was untrue.

I was not so sure, for the entire brigade had come to Thalassa at various times for drinks, and had done themselves proud on us. But of course I dare not say a thing.

"Why the hell did you let Nic pay?" he asked, "I would never have done so."

I could well believe that one!

But in the morning I found what a beautiful and picturesque town Falmouth was. It was rhododendron time, and the hills were turned to rose and vermilion with them. Mercifully the maids liked it, too, though poor Fanthorpe thought nothing of the Cornish oven, which was a pig! The place had charm. Every afternoon a band played in the park sprawling before our windows. You would never have thought a war was on, and there was no sound of gunfire at sea.

But how casual they were about the lights! This sent me into agonies of intense apprehension (coming from the East coast, where it was dark as death and we were always having scares,) I asked one of the officers if he thought that it was safe, and he was almost amused! Of course it was safe! The old Hun had got insufficient steam to get as far as Falmouth, and there would never be so much as a hiccough from them.

Then one evening, when we were in the middle of those delicious strawberry and cream dinners at the Greenbanks Hotel (which stands at the far end of the harbour), there came the sudden violent crack of a terrific explosion! Then gunfire! Apparently a submarine had appeared from somewhere unknown and was, as Arthur said, having a bit of fun!' It put the fear of God into those who had thought that we were so safe.

After that, they darkened down a little (nothing like the East coast of course), but better than it had been before.

I liked Falmouth, but Arthur was restless. Poor man, he felt entirely defeated by the lost pip, and that was reasonable. He had come under a cloud, as we all knew, of course, and heaven only knows the sort of report which Conky had sent on ahead of him. My concern was that nobody appreciated the fact that he was ill. He was losing weight, getting wildly depressed at times, and then drank more to cheer himself up, which was understandable. What we both wanted to do was to bring some influence to bear (the family seemed to have lots of this) and get him a post in London. He was quite unfit to be living as he was, driven from pillar to post, and I wanted if I could, to get him out of Mess life. His friends were his worst enemies, if one can put it that way, but it happened to be true.

I had arranged for Prescott Hedley – the top gynaecologist – to look after me with the baby; and Rosie Vanderpump, who had nursed Mrs Franklin next door to me in Frinton, was coming on the first of October wherever I happened to be. She was a very nice person, and Mrs Franklin had had four babies with her, and gave her a strong recommendation. I could only pray that I should not be stuck down at Falmouth, because I thought that if this happened, I should go mad.

The doctor who we had disliked Arthur, but was very kind to me, and most concerned about everything. I wrote to my Mother-in-law urging her to hurry things up, but either she never got the letter, or she did not bother to write back, for I got no answer.

Then one day, out of the blue, as maybe these things always do it happened.

Arthur had been getting much worse. Now he would go on

duty at dawn and flop out before the troops. They always said that he had fainted. What *did* one do? Then quite suddenly dear Uncle Billy put out a hand, and he got an appointment in London with the Ministry of Pensions. I remember bursting into tears for the sheer relief of it all.

This meant an office job for Arthur, I never quite knew how they got it for him but being a parson's daughter, I did believe that this was the answer to prayer.

The maids stayed behind to tidy up, and then follow us on next week, by which time we should have got a furnished house somewhere, as handy for the Ministry as possible.

We went up to London, and Arthur got in touch with the Galers immediately. On the Sunday we went down to tea with them in Dulwich, and Hugh Galer, had sighted a furnished house to let further along the Croxted Road. So they went off together to have a look at it. When they returned, they had actually taken it without my even seeing it – and I was the one who had to run the wretched place, I was most annoyed by it.

Even worse, a little later that week, Hugh sent in a bill "for services rendered", which I thought was utterly abominable! We could have taken it ourselves, and would have done. Arthur said he was a hard-up old friend. I was not pacified. I said that when I found Thalassa at Frinton nobody had paid me a shilling for it, and I should not have taken it even if they had offered.

I did not like the Galers, who seemed to have done remarkably well out of the Denham-Cookes at various times. Even if they had got Arthur into Cambridge (for which indeed they did deserve their fees) trying to get something for going over a furnished house to let with him *was* a bit too much.

We moved in almost at once, in the August, with the baby due in the October. Also at this time Hugh Galer had told me of a doctor living in Brixton who could help us with Arthur's condition.

The three of us went to see him. It was an awful old-fashioned house, over-crowded with poor furniture, and I should think that it had not had a window open in it for years. It was in the Brixton Road.

The interview was not very satisfactory. Too much depended

on whether Arthur would stop taking the stuff or not. Nobody seemed to realize that he could not control himself, and needed help; not reproof which would never persuade him to do what they asked.

The new house was pleasant: morning-room and dining-room in front, and a drawing-room at the back, opening with French windows into the little garden. It was nothing like Thalassa, of course, though it had six bedrooms, but I was so thankful to have found the place where the baby would be born. That was all-important to me, for time was getting short.

We dined fairly often at the R.A.C., and whenever I went back to the car, it was always to find that it was loaded up with gin and brandy, which somehow or other he and Barker, the chauffeur, had contrived to get on board. I wanted to keep a private check on how much he drank, but this was impossible, however much the doctors wanted it.

Then suddenly he collapsed. He passed out in a dead faint, and the doctors got him into King's College Hospital. Mercifully it happened within a few hours of Nurse Vanderpump's arrival, so that I was not alone. The baby was now due, but did not appear. I must say that this tardiness of the child was a help, for his father recovered somewhat before he was born. They got him better. There was a young parson in the same ward to whom I owe my undying thanks, for he was so good to him. He was one of the few men to whom one did not have to explain everything, for he understood. In a way the baby's delay was most fortunate, for in early November Arthur had progressed sufficiently to enable him to come home to tea.

This time I did manage to convince Mr Hedley that the baby was late, really late, and he came to see me and arranged to operate next day. Something had got to be done.

To cheer myself up that afternoon, when I had got rid of him I went off to a sale at the Brixton Bon Marché, with my ever bright eye for a bargain! I might look awful – and I did –, but I got some glorious bargains. Coming home, to my surprise I started to cry. Usually I am not very good at crying, being too much of a fighter for that! The kind nurse suggested that I went early to bed, so after Arthur had come to tea and had left again, I had an early dinner and a nice leisurely bath, and got into bed. It was then that I felt very odd indeed, in a way that I had never felt before. I fetched the nurse. The baby had been coming for a good twelve hours, and I had not had a clue!

When I think of what the Bon Marché had been saved, I do bless my lucky stars! Mr Hedley arrived before midnight, and I had a bedroom prepared for him, so that if he wished he could get some sleep. Everybody was very kind.

I had insisted on the treatment then very fashionable, known as Twilight Sleep. I believe that it has died out today, which is a pity, for I must say that it was remarkably efficient with me. I know that next day, when Mr Hedley asked me if I could remember anything of it, all I could recall was that I had seen him go to my handkerchief drawer and take out of it some chocolates that I had stored away there! I hardly dared tell him this, it did not seem very polite, so I just said, "Oh no, nothing at all," but I do remember him eating my chocolates!

It would have been a dark dawn when they brought me round. I was in no pain, and there were three doctors in the room at the time. They asked me if I would be very disappointed if the baby was dead. I said they must do what they could, and then again lost consciousness.

Two hours later I came to with Mr Hedley holding my hand and saying "It's a boy, and a whopper!"

The whopper was a 'breech', eleven and a half pounds of him!

He was red-headed like my father, and there was something of my father in his face. Arthur was enchanted with a son, and bought expensive presents for everyone save myself. Mrs Denham-Cookes, who had been convinced from the first that I should produce a daughter, had gone rather quiet. Two evenings later, Chown the butler arrived with flowers for me, and I insisted that he should be brought up to my room to see "the little master", as he called him. He went over to the cot and inspected the baby, and was so nice about it. There was no sign of a malformed hand.

My sister-in-law never came near, and my mother-in-law followed her example. Then when she heard that the butler had been in my bedroom (which was the way in which she put it), she was furiously angry. I came to the conclusion that there are some people whom you cannot please, and that is that.

I was annoyed that Arthur gave the nurse a rather lovely brooch, and some bracelets went into the kitchen, and something to the chauffeur, but I got absolutely nothing.

I understood that it was probable that Arthur would not return into the army; he might be retired. Just before I was fully recovered, he was dispatched to a famous nursing-home just outside Edinburgh, of all places, where they dealt with his kind of malady. But I need not have been dismayed, for Craiglockhart worked the miracle, for which I was undyingly grateful. He hated the place, of course, but I should have expected that. His army career came to an end, for he was invalided out. That part of our married life had gone for ever.

When he returned just before Christmas, he was very much changed; less on edge, his skin had become clear, his rather pretty eyes were bright, and emotionally he was far quieter. His mother, who had never once rung up in his absence, rang now through Rowland the maid, who said that Mrs Denham-Cookes wished to see him. I suggested that we took the baby along, but this got a very cold reception. Obviously she did not wish to see him.

Arthur knew that he could drink only milk; he must have a tremendous amount of it, and whatever happened, no spirits. I think that I had a tragic inkling that something could go wrong, and I made him promise that he would stick to milk. I knew that Mrs Denham-Cookes would think it very "common", and would say that it was my idea, but he *must* stick to it.

He went up to see her.

Two hours later, Chown rang up in some consternation. Mrs Denham-Cookes would be very glad if I would fetch my husband home, because he was not feeling at all well, and they had sent the car for me. I think I knew then. I went stone cold all over. He had gone off fairly happily, hoping to get a fat cheque out of Ma, as he put it.

On the step I realized that I was trembling, and when Chown answered the door he looked exactly like a ghost.

"What has happened?" I asked.

Like all good butlers, he sheered off giving away anything. "The Captain is in the library, madam," was all that I could get out of him.

He escorted me to the library, and I knew that every step alarmed me, and I did not know what to do next. Mrs Denham-Cookes, complete with ear trumpet, sat there in her usual chair, and she was apparently unmoved. She said that Arthur was upsetting her and she wanted me to take him home. He was lying on the hearthrug, apparently unconscious. She said that they had had a row, I gathered that he had been furiously angry with her, and suspected that she had again threatened to stop his allowance, for she always did this when she wanted to be annoying. He had been very rude, she said, because so far she had not seen the baby.

I asked "What do I do?"

"You can't leave him here," she said.

I knelt down beside him. He smelt strongly of whisky, and I knew that she had given him some and undone all the good that Craiglockhart had done. I knew then that the bright dream of recovery had died. I only thanked God that Mother would never know (poor thing, it would have worried her to death.)

Chown and I got him on to his feet, and in the end into the hall and to the car which was waiting for us. When we got back to Dulwich my own chauffeur helped me. But it was one of the most ghastly drives of all my life, knowing that a dream had died, knowing that this was the end, and that he would never be himself again in the same way.

That night I cried myself to sleep.

8

FROM DEATH TO LIFE

We returned to Frinton to the house called Poona, early in the new year. I took a furnished house meanwhile to give us time to straighten Poona out, and the furnished house was next door to Gladys Cooper's.

I wanted to get Arthur away from his mother, because she was certainly no help to him, and at times made him wretched, always threatening to stop the allowance if he did not do what she wanted. It would be better to do without her, I felt, and get away from her eternal threats.

We moved into the new home in the February. It was a small house with five bedrooms and a charming bathroom. Downstairs there was a dining-room on the right, and his study on the left, with the drawing-room running along the back, leading into a conservatory which I adored. He liked it too.

Quietly I went on with my writing, for this was a great comfort to me during a period when I was living under severe strain. He detested my writing books, and I had to destroy each one as I finished it. But he loved the garden and I found that he had never before seen a flower grow. He could not believe that he could plant anything. His mother told him one had to be a gardener to do it. It was pathetic how he had been brought up, pathetic that he knew so little, and how his life had been so wasted!

In the spring of 1918, I wanted a second child for the sake of Pip, my small son. Arthur did not want this. He seemed now to be lost in a sea of helpless confusion. He was in a way 'drifting', and, try as I would, there was nothing that I could do to stop it.

Luckily he had an old friend who had been at Trinity Hall

with him, Herman Rogers-Tillstone. Herman had gone in for law, had a break-down, and then went in for medicine. He used to come to stay at times, because Arthur was a very great strain for me, and this gave me a rest. I found that I relied on Herman; at least he knew everything about the conditions. We both knew that Arthur was going downhill. We both wanted desperately to help him, and there was just nothing that could be done.

* * *

In the early autumn of 1918 that shocking plague which was called 'Spanish Flu' suddenly swept through Europe. It was ghastly, and the people living today have no idea how shocking it was!

You met people in the morning, and by the evening you were told that they were dead. I had it quite slightly, and recovered, then the cook got it, and she got it badly, poor thing! The nurse had it next, and then Arthur. He was, of course, in no condition to fight it.

He became semi-conscious, at times raving. Then his mother was helpful, and sent down Sir Thomas Parkinson to see him. He was a charming man, helpful, and most kind about it coming into my life at an agonizing moment when I needed kindness.

He was not hopeful, and thought I ought to have somebody else here with me. He wondered if Kitty could come? The thought of having Kitty horrified me. As far as I could see she had never grown-up, a woman with a child's mind, someone whom in the village we would have classed as being 'slightly mental'. I felt that he did not hold out much hope, but he changed the whole routine and ordered him a whisky straight away, and this did help him.

The rest is like some hideous dream, too bad to be true. In ten days I lost over a stone in weight. We had a nurse, but often had to get men from the R.A.M.C. to help us, for he was fighting at moments and more than a woman could manage. During the last few hours Herman came from Norwich and he was goodness itself. Towards the end, poor Arthur ceased fighting, and lapsed into peaceful unconsciousness. Although I longed for him to speak to me again, I did feel it was perhaps easier for him if quietly, without knowing anything more about it, he went. Gently he slept out of a world that had never been too good to him. The shame was that I had come into his life too late to save him from himself.

Herman and I went down into his library and sat there. Fanthorpe had got up. She made some coffee and brought it to us. I do hope that I was not too much trouble to them both, but I felt appalled. I had done everything that I could to save him, and now he had died in my arms.

Herman said that as soon as was possible he must ring up Prince's Gate. He thought that it was better for him to tell them than for me. When he did ring, Rowland, who was my mother-in-law's personal maid, answered the 'phone. He asked to speak to my sister-in-law. Rowland said that on no account could she be disturbed. Herman finally turned angry, he said that she had got to be disturbed, for the matter was urgent. In the end Rowland reluctantly gave way, and Kitty came to the 'phone. First of all he told her that Arthur was worse, and then she flew into a temper, and said what was the good of worrying her, for she couldn't do anything. At this hour of the morning, too!

"Why bother me?" she asked. "I can't do anything."

He was furiously angry with her, and flashed back "Your brother is dead. He died just before three this morning. Now go and tell your mother," then he slammed down the receiver.

I thought it a dreadful scene, but I did realize how he felt, understandable after everything that we had been through. Ten minutes later she rang up again. She had told her mother, who did not believe a word that we had said, but she would send down Mr Levett, the solicitor, and he would find out what it was all about! I must admit that 'Rog-Till' was then really nasty. He let fly, and quietly I fainted.

Mr Levett arrived just before midday, met by Rog-Till. He apologized! They had not realized that it was serious: No, nobody would be coming to the funeral, which would be a military one. He was not very sympathetic. Rog-Till was frank with him. He said, "You don't seem to think of what that girl has been through, do you?"

Mr Levett said he was sorry for me, but he could not have helped, anyway.

"They're all mad," Rog-Till said, and when he found Fanthorpe hanging about to know if Mr Levett would be staying to lunch, he said. "No. He isn't getting any lunch out of us. He can go elsewhere!"

I thought it awful, but did agree.

It was then that I found the nursery empty. It was Fanthorpe who told me. Last night Stanley Nicholson from Walton (who had a small son the same age) had fetched away my baby and his nannie, because he thought they would be better out of it. It was *most* helpful and kind! I could not have thanked him sufficiently.

He spoke to me on the telephone. "They are quite all right," he said, "don't worry about it. We'll keep them both as long as ever you want."

None of the family came to the funeral, and I myself could not go. There were heaps of flowers, heaps of loving messages, but oh, how much better it would have been if some of them had helped the poor man! None of them had tried to save him.

I went back to Norwich with Rog-Till when it was over. He wanted me to get out of the house. He was very very good to me, arranging for the furniture to be moved round before I returned, so that I should come back to a different background. I felt quite helplessly alone. I suppose death was the sole way out, but he was only twenty-five. The day of life had been too short for him, and the night of death would be too long. He had been the victim of other people, and I could not help him. It was horrifying.

Picking up the pieces was not easy. I was greatly helped by dear Edith Horton, who lived next door to me. Her own marriage had broken, and she had returned to live with a difficult mother and a dying father. Her only son had been killed in the war last year; she had known endless trouble, poor thing, and was quite the kindest woman I have ever met.

When the spring came, it was she who insisted on my getting out and about again. It was she who got me into V.A.D. uniform.

Phyllis Holman ran a wonderful Home for seriously wounded

officers, in London, and she opened up a seaside branch in Frinton. She took Turret Lodge, which was a very large house on the front, and the idea was to give her patients a short time by the sea. We had Sister-in-charge, who had been widowed in the war, there were two male nurses, and the rest of us were V.A.D.s. I was patient, kind-hearted, and did not shrink from hard work, for I had learnt a lot in my father's parish, and I must say that Sister got as much as she could out of me.

But being a V.A.D. was an enormous help, as possibly Hortie had known it would be. The officers were mostly hopelessly wounded, yet young enough to get themselves into all sorts of trouble. In Frinton we had the Queen's Hotel, but no common-or-garden pub. They had these, and in numbers, over at Walton, a mile and a half away; I have never seen a place with so many pubs. When nobody was looking, they would 'phone Race and Scott for a cab, and slip out and shoot over to Walton, with about four legs amongst three of them. Once or twice I had to go over there and fetch them back.

"Men!" said Sister in a fury, "They drive me mad."

In the real hard work which the Home offered I found my own self again, for I had suffered badly. When the lease ran out, I was sorry. The party returned to London.

Joscelyn returned from Egypt in the mid-July. How satisfying it was to have someone of one's own flesh and blood here with one! He looked brown and sunburnt, better that I had ever seen him before. I got new plain clothes for him, and later, when he had had a bit of a holiday, he would get a job.

That was the summer when Frinton brimmed with the famous. Winston Churchill was here, and the Prince of Wales, and there were dances every night somewhere. I think that Joscelyn must have found the life unsettling, and he was worried about getting the right job, which was every young man's bother. In the long run, I persuaded him to develop his art, for he painted very well, as my father did. He went to St Martin's School of Art. But my main worry was my trustees. Mr Nicholson told me, and with truth, that I should never get real help from that quarter.

I came back to my pen.

If Frinton thought I should marry again all in five months (I was told there was heavy betting at the golf club) they were entirely wrong. That was the last thing that I wished to do. I started in Fleet Street. I worked for an established author called Calder Wilson. He was a strange man, excellent at plots, but he could not put them down, and he had two collaborators, Nellie Tom-Gallon and myself. Ultimately this brought me into Arthur Pearson's office, sent for to an interview with Mr Lamburn, then editor of *Pearson's Weekly*. That was the door opened for me! I had thrust my way into the smaller magazines, and quietly I was writing a novel in my spare time, which I sold to Hutchinson, and got a contract. I remember when I received it, looking at it as if the words were magic!

If Frinton had bet heavily on my re-marriage they had put their money on the wrong woman, because I had other ideas! Now I wanted my own life in my own way. The world was my oyster.

Behind it all I had for some time been worried about my father, for I had no news of him. He had married Josephine Sims, and had then disappeared. By chance I was told that he had an office in Holborn, and one day I went there to see him. He looked much older, of course, and I knew by his appearance that he was working hard and had been through difficult times. But so had I. He flew at me, saying that it was all my fault, but in the end admitted that he had behaved disgracefully to my mother, not even attending the funeral.

He was interested in his grandson, and came down to Frinton to see him. I visited him in Balham where he was living, and met Josephine for the first time. It is, of course, always difficult to appreciate what one's father sees in another woman, but she was limp, a poor wizened little thing, and apparently his great trouble was that she was fond of drink.

It was now that, according to Mr Nicholson's always good advice, I built a little bungalow – it cost £600 – in Pole Barn Lane, definitely not the best end of Frinton, but land was cheaper there. Arthur had not left me well-off. I should have about £700 a year until his mother died, and then thousands, provided that I did not re-marry.

I liked the bungalow, but after a couple of years I found the

journey to London tiring. I had a good offer for the house, sold
it, and then had to find somewhere else, at a time when there was
not the hint of a home anywhere. But I had luck. My brother and
I, on motor bike and side-car, went round outer London
searching, and we came to Harlow, then a small village with a
good train service. I went over a lovely old Jacobean house, or
rather half of it, for it had been split into two. There were three
sitting-rooms and nine bedrooms, I made a bid for it, and got it.

Harlow would be easier for Joscelyn at St Martin's School, and
a shorter journey for me. There was also at that time Harlow
College, where Pip could start his pre-prep. career.

The work was improving, and the books were selling. I liked
working for Walter Hutchinson. Everybody said that he was
mad, but he and I got on very well.

I went down to Plymouth for a change of air, after the move. I
went because the *Royal Oak* was there. I knew one of the officers
and could be entertained. This was a mistake, for, when I got
there, the man in question immediately proposed, and I told him
that I had no intention of re-marrying. He was furious with me.
It was the day he had a friend in to tea, Gower Robinson, quite a
different type, and one of those men who had never spelt a word
wrong in his life, which fascinated me!

I liked life aboard ship, dancing and talking. They never
understood how I drank water, or, if rash, a ginger-beer, which
was *not* like themselves at all. Gower Robinson never pressed me
to drink something that I did not want. He came ashore to see me
later in the week, when I was having a lot of trouble with the
other naval officer, who was now threatening to shoot himself.
I must say that Gower handled the situation very well, he was a
great help. He then asked me to go down to Cowes a little later
on, for the *Royal Oak* was to be the guard-ship at Cowes Week,
and he would love to entertain me.

It was not good weather, but utterly thrilling. On the
Thursday they gave an enormous dance, which meant of course
that I did not see as much of Robbie as I had hoped to do, and far
too much of the other officer, who was now telling me that he
would cut his throat, leaving behind him a note blaming me.

By the night of the dance, it had rained all the afternoon,

worrying them about the state of the deck, but when I arrived on board the ship looked like fairyland. It is ghastly to think of her submerged hulk in Scapa Flow, and I do think of her.

Robbie wrote in his diary:

6th August 1925. Cowes.
Thank heaven it is over! It poured all day until five, and the decks were swimming, but with radiators and yard-arm group we got it dry. Frightfully busy all day, but I was rewarded, for the dance was a huge success. I managed to sit out half a dozen dances with Ursula, who is a very lovable child. She is so spontaneously happy, and seemed to be enjoying herself. Thank God she is, it's about the first time in her life.

Maybe he had got something there, though child or no child, I knew a great deal more about life that he ever did. He seemed to be running everything at Cowes (they do work their men) and he asked me later to go down to Sheerness because there he would be freer and we could talk. I did like visiting ships! People were nice to me, and the fact that I had just managed to get some foothold on the ladder of literature made things easier. I was still young enough to want happiness, and my life had hardly brimmed over with it.

I went to Sheerness for the week-end. This is Robbie's diary at the time.

Sheerness. 10th August. 1925
Ursula came on board to tea, and I went to the Fountain to have dinner with her and had a lovely evening. God give me strength to ask her to be Mrs C.G.R.!

On the next day he did it!

Sheerness. 20th August 1925
Oh, what a wonderful day! I plucked up courage to ask her, and after a bit of indecision, she said yes. I want to bounce and sing, and whistle for joy. Previously I had lunch with her, and won the doubles tournament with Everett. We nearly got beaten in the semi-final, but in the final easily won. Ursula dined on board.

I had found Robbie to be the most reliable man in my life. If he did a job, he did it well, and I admired that, also I was wretchedly lonely. I and my brother had never got on very well together, though I would never have let him down and was doing everything that I could to get him properly established in life.

I needed someone to back me up. Most people in my life had been most undependable. My father had for ever been in some trouble, and then came my difficult, and at times horrifying, marriage, and widowhood. I told Robbie that on re-marriage I should lose my interest in Colonel Denham-Cookes' estate, but this did not seem to worry him at all. He told me that he had prospects from his people, though what on earth they were I never discovered, and of course would have been mere chicken feed, even if they had existed, compared to what I should have inherited.

But money is not everything.

Next day he hired a car and took me to that delightful little village of Otford, where they had lived for some time. His mother had died from the same trouble as mine. I could not find out much about them, for they were not an emotional family at all. In his diary he writes of that day:

Sheerness. 21st August 1925.
Landed at 11.30 and had lunch with Ursula at the Fountain. After that we took a car over to Otford and had tea with Dad. What a heavenly kid she is, and so brave over telling me things! The drive was gorgeous, though she was afraid of meeting Dad.

Otford was one of the sweetest little Kentish villages, not over-built then, and standing in a beautiful valley, with a ruined castle in it that had had something to do with King Henry VIII. Robbie's father had been a stockbroker, now retired.

I was a little worried, I admit. They had originally lived in the Old Parsonage, but now they lived in a tiny house which was enchanting, and the garden of great charm. But they were not the same sort of people as the Denham-Cookes at all. When his uncle on the maternal side (he lived with them) came in, I admit that I really *was* disturbed. In those days one's sense of status was far more important than it is now, and this man, although he was doing his best to be kind, was a 'funny' man.

I *can't* do it, I thought.

Already I was deeply fond of Gower, and knew he had no idea how I felt. Naturally one accepts one's own people: for one is brought up with them. I could not possibly tell him how I felt, because these were *his* people, and of course he loved them. His father was hampered by being extremely deaf, (but thank heaven not with an ear trumpet, like Mrs Denham-Cookes). His uncle was an odd little man, I am sure that he meant well, but he was *not* quite what I had expected.

Could I possibly go on with this?

Undoubtedly Robbie's home was insignificant, nothing like Whitchurch had been, and most certainly not like Prince's Gate. His people were very ordinary, I would not dare to have thought what they did three generations back. But Robbie was such a dear kind person! What I wondered was, could we *afford* to marry? He told me he would come into all they had got, (but *what* had they got?) It seemed to me that they were all existing on a knife-edge. I had done it so long myself that I recognized the motions!

I had come to the conclusion that I could not go on as a widow for ever, for although Joscelyn and I never quarrelled, we had so little in common. Perhaps it was my fault and I never understood him, who knows? Robbie told me that he would have sufficient (and I am sure that he did think that), but I was looking ahead. This is not security, I told myself.

I think that his father had done fairly well on the Stock Exchange, but in the last part of his life he developed that curious habit lots of old people do develop, of going down the village street and giving away five pound notes to any 'poor old dear' who told him a hard-luck story! When he died there was practically nothing save a house, which we could not sell for love or money.

What do I *do*? I asked myself.

I don't think Robbie noticed a thing, because of course it was his background, and one does not see things in one's own people. Later he came down to stay at Harlow with me, and fell in love with Epping Forest, which is so glorious.

The Dower House made no impression on him, even if it had

space, — big comfortable sprawling rooms and nine bedrooms. We discussed the future. I was anxious for Joscelyn. As the *Oak* was going out to the Mediterranean for three years, the marriage should make no change for my brother, who could go on living with me.

My father came down to meet Gower, and they got on well, but instantly my father made enquiries of me about the other side, his home, his people, his expectations. He said, "Well, it is for you to make up your mind, you know."

His father was a charmer, and always most kind to me, and I liked his Aunt Emma, a lady dedicated to good works and shocked because I fetched eggs from a farm on a Sunday! But we got on well together and liked each other immensely.

That was a rush of an autumn, for I had a book to finish, and at the end of November we married.

I admit that I had found the last years of widowhood very dull, and I longed for a companion. I had too much responsibility of course, combined with my own launching out into Fleet Street. Perhaps every bride has this faintly underlying sense of anxiety. Perhaps too much had already gone wrong in my life for me ever to think something could go right for a change. I was worried.

I knew that Robbie was the most trustworthy man that I had ever met. He talked so kindly. He said I had become so accustomed to Fate playing tricks on me that I always expected another one, and life is not like that really.

"It has made you suspicious," and he laughed. "We will have to put that right."

* * *

We were married early on a November morning, in the old church at Harlow, and although we had meant to spend the honeymoon there, everything went so wrong, that in the end we actually did a bolt! The cook had an accident with a tin of something, and we had to get the doctor to her. It was not too bad, and next morning we left Joscelyn in charge and nipped up to London to the Great Eastern Hotel, where I knew the manager and got a nice room quite easily.

We spent the leave going to theatres galore, for we both adored them. It was different from his usual leaves spent in 'doing the garden' at home. It was pleasant, and before we joined the ship at Sheerness, we spent a couple of nights at Otford. I liked my father-in-law, but felt that somehow there was a wall between us! I found Uncle Sidney tiresome; I am never very fond of the professional wit, but I did start a new book which is always my refuge in an emergency.

Thank God that the love of writing is such a strong driving force, which has helped me round many a corner in a difficult life. I have shed bitter tears over it at times but the fact that it is there is eternally an immense help. It opens the door on a new world. It is *joy*!

We went off to Sheerness together, I to the hotel, he on board hoping to return for dinner that night.

Now I had known army wives, I thought there was not that much difference between the two services, when it came to the women, but how wrong I was! I know my father had told me, "Don't forget that the Naval wife is far more R.N. than her husband is! Do remember that one," and I learnt it the very first night at Sheerness. But one thing I determined: This remark would never apply to me, because, thank God, I was not born grand.

We motored down to the Fountain Hotel which looks out on to that dismal dockyard wall (hardly a pleasant view) but I must say that it is handy for the ships. Officers were allowed to sleep ashore if they were married (privately I am sure there were quite a lot of them who did it without being married, boys being boys!) On the first night Robbie had found much more to do on board than he had anticipated, so he stayed to catch up, and I had dinner alone.

I was walking calmly into the dining-room when a rather plain, unknown woman, who had been coming along behind me, caught at my arm. She said that she believed her husband was senior to mine. I said, "So what?" She was obviously annoyed, as this apparently meant that she was senior to me, and therefore walked in first! I looked at her, and I must say that I hate to think of how I looked, and then walked straight in in

front of her. My feelings were that we might as well kick off on
the right foot, and this was an ordinary hotel, where people went
in as they wished, or so I imagined.

When Robbie arrived, I told him about it, and he was most
indignant, then he admitted that I might find some of them "a bit
snooty", but this was an everyday hotel and, as far as he knew,
there was no seniority amongst the wives. How wrong he was!

When I went up to the drawing-room afterwards for coffee, I
found that unbeknownst to a stranger, they had made the most
curious arrangement of chairs and sofas, so that junior wives sat
here, and the senior wives sat there! I had no idea which I was!

I was furious when a fat woman started the conversation by
saying, "Now that you have joined the Service, of course you
will give up your writing."

I said, "Certainly not! Why should I?"

Perhaps few people realize that this gift is life itself. I would
give up almost everything else in the world for my pen! She
adopted the attitude of "Well of course you'll have to," which
got no encouragement from me.

I had to ignore them. In the long run I settled this argument for
good, because I published one of the best books I have ever
written, called *The Log of an N.O.'s Wife*. This was illustrated by
Charles Graves, Walter Hutchinson published it. He was
enchanted to do it, for this was just the time when his first wife
ran off with a Naval Officer, and he felt about the Royal Navy
very much the way that I did! The book was rude, but it was
true. It hit them much harder than they could hit back – I saw to
that –, because the pen can bite. The publication ran through
three editions in a fortnight, for, strangely enough, I was not the
first person in this world who had thought they were difficult.
Once and for all I settled that we-know-everything attitude to
life!

It was in the January that we parted for the first time, and,
believe me, Sheerness dockyard is not a very sympathetic place. I
was shocked at the weeping wives collected there to say adieu to
husbands who had to be aboard by midnight. I walked back
alone to the hotel. It was a ghastly moment.

In the January, I went to sea for the first time in my whole life to join him out in Gib. I drove down to the coast with a grim feeling of apprehension in my heart, Joscelyn driving me. I went aboard, and never knew the actual moment when we started, because I had sat down to a very good lunch.

When we turned out into the sea itself, it was none too calm, and although I tried to spot the places that I knew along the coast, it was not easy, because everything looks so very different. We had a fairly rough journey, and I felt quite ill at moments, not actually sick, but most apprehensive. But I was determined not to let the side down, for I felt this was what I should be doing if I were sick, and I turned up bravely for all meals. I admit that I could not eat much, but I managed to put the face on it that I thought the Royal Navy would expect of me!

When we came out of the bay off Portugal, it suddenly became warm and lovely, like spring! I have never forgotten the joy of that first radiant sunshine. We were due into Gib. about nine in the morning, so I made sure and got myself called at five. I did not intend to be late on this. Nothing would have stopped me from seeing the Rock come into sight, and my entry into what was to me a brand new world.

Here it was spring!

The officer of the watch was a very dark young man, not much older than myself, and he seemed to feel much the same way. Seeing me on deck (the only one) he did express some surprise, and came along to see if he could be helpful. This, so I imagined was the last thing that he wanted to be, though he did get me a cup of hot coffee, which was lovely.

I was keenly interested in Tarifa, a sprawling little town on the sea-edge to my left. He told me that it was nothing much, and later, when I visited it with a Spanish journalist, I found that he was quite right, for the mayor received me with no shoes on, and a pair of trousers that could never have passed muster in England.

I shall never forget the supreme thrill when that giant Rock slowly came into sight! It was much bigger than I had expected, far more vivid, too, for I was comparing it with Meon Hill, and the Cotswolds. In truth I had lived such a simple and such a limited life. How great it was, and how powerful! It was all so blue, and so warmly lovely, I told myself. Coming nearer, it got taller still. We turned very slowly into the harbour. It is strange how, when a ship slows down, and the engines have stopped the growl to which you are accustomed (for it is some sort of background music), then they go *piano*! The ship moved more gently. Apparently officials had to come aboard before we could go ashore and they went down to the captain's cabin, where I imagine they had this and that.

Again, but very slowly, we went forward. The Rock towered over us on the right, magnificently strong, and beside the shore I saw an almond tree, rosy with blossom, and could not believe it to be true. I had left winter behind me in England.

"It's heaven!" I told the officer of the watch, who I am sure should have been doing other things than talking to me.

"That's what you think about it now, but it isn't much of a place, as you'll find later on," was his reply.

We dropped anchor.

Instantly the sea became alive with little boats which were speeding towards us. They darted in and out of the Home Fleet and the Mediterranean Fleet, meeting here for the annual spring cruise. There seemed to be hundreds of ships, all freshly painted, or so they looked, spick and span and highly polished, each exactly at its right anchorage. What a magnificent sight they were! And today ... but don't let's think of that!

Robbie came off in a picket boat to fetch me, and I went down the side to it. The whole of my arrival had been the most wonderful experience, something that I would not have missed for the world. We went ashore, and he got a *carroza*, again something new to me, and it looked most dangerous. I regarded it with nervous apprehension, for it seemed as if you could never possibly stay in it. It is very flimsy, low to the ground, no doors, and with a canopy looped over it to make it look like a travelling four-post bed!

"Oh, I can't possibly go in THAT!" I said.

"Come on. It's quite all right," said Robbie. I got in most reluctantly, it seemed to be so very gimcrack, and we went bowling up the street to the Hotel Cecil.

It was then that I realized life had opened a new door – for me, on a world I had never thought of seeing. That afternoon I flung off my coat as we sat in the *Alameda*, with all sorts of strange flowers around us, and the strong sweet scent of it all. The Barbary apes came down into the trees, and fascinated me. Later in the week we went up to the Rock, right to the top, and surely it has the most breath-taking view I had as yet ever seen.

The whole visit was unique to me.

My life changed then! Here were cypresses, azaleas, and orange blossom, and wistaria all together, and it enchanted me. But perhaps I am one of those people who are born with a cloud in their sky. Ever since I was a small child and first caught my father kissing some woman who was not my mother, and telling me "to keep the secret", life has gone in an odd fashion for me. Nothing can ever be completely as it happens to other people. This is not imagination; it is, unhappily, the cruel truth, and although one tries to draw down the curtain over it, (as one conceals a death) it does not always work.

I can never forget attempting to shelter my father at the rectory, or the sheer agony of finding that my mother had cancer. Those were years when all the time we were living with an enemy. Then the two years married to Arthur, who could be so dear to me, and all the time fighting the enemy which was killing him. I always have to fight some enemy not of my own making but ever there.

I had come to Fleet Street, and that is no playground. I loved the hard work of it, but it can be bitterly disappointing of course, and you have to take this as it comes.

I had always told myself that I should never marry again, and then I had done. Robbie and I loved each other deeply and with complete trust. We were intensely happy. I do not think that I could have gone on living without him, but behind him lay that something that was so different. Not all of us are made to pattern.

Robbie was by far the nicest man I had ever met, but most conventional, and I am not! His people had never entertained, whereas mine had. He had gone to Dover College, where undoubtedly (if they had taken girls) I should have been at the bottom of the form. That was unless I had got annoyed about it, and then I should have worked like a black, for I do this rather well when enraged. He had never had girl-friends, and when I said that I thought he must have missed a lot of fun, he seemed surprised. His life had been something of a 'flat calm' as they call it in the Service, but maybe the 'flat calm' is easier to live with, than the one which gives you gale warnings.

Robbie knew very little of life. He did not dance and our existences had been the exact opposites. His had been something of a 'hermit childhood', I had never been able to cram sufficient into mine.

Now life had opened a new door for me, and a miracle had come about, for I was in love with life!

I went along to Malta at just one hour's notice, for in the Royal Navy you have to learn to pack quickly, one hour and you are off to sea again! This time it was a small boat; I doubt if she was really seaworthy, and she was run by a ghastly old captain There were five N.O.s' wives, following along to Malta, and all but myself had brought their skipping ropes! I thought they were trying to be funny when they told me, but every morning they skipped together in a corner of the deck. "Must have exercise," said the R.N. wives.

I wrote a book (and did a lot of it, too) but there was an officer aboard us who loathed the captain, found that I did, and so came and sat with me, a great deterrent to the book.

We had breakfast of steak and onions at 6 a.m., some ghastly coffee at ten, lunch (more steak and onions) at midday, and high tea. That was a glorious trip!

Off Tunis something went wrong, and they were rather worried about the lifeboats, (which apparently nobody had looked at for ages) and they were not quite sure that they could work properly. "And with those damned women on board!" said the old captain.

I was not worried, for the sea was calm, and I could swim that distance, we were only about a mile off the shore, so that would not have been too much. However, we pottered into Malta a day late.

Malta at that time was wildly attractive, but of course it is so bare. It was not over-built then; today I believe that it is one vast town, and we explored all over it. But I got ill out there, —

apparently it does this to some people. You can or you cannot, take it.

Happiest of all the places that we visited was Venice, for the *Eagle* in which my husband was now serving, took out the 'planes for the coming Schneider Cup race. Benice was *en fête*. That morning they talked of nothing else, and then when we won the race they dropped it like a stone! That is the way that foreigners behave. We went to Brioni, today unknown, but then it was a lovely little island, where there was a tremendous lot of polo. There were no houses, only two enormous hotels on it. Pip, aged about ten, came with me, and I was landed in Venice where I took a boat to Brioni, whilst Pip went on there in his step-father's ship. I got there first, and a shocking boat that was! I had booked a most smelly little cabin, and so had a stout American gentleman, who would not give it up, so I slept on deck, on a coil of rope, and paid to do it. Can you believe it?

I got there at teatime, the *Eagle* not yet in, and went ashore to the marvellous hotel, the best in which I have ever stayed. I sat down to tea on the terrace with a horde of Americans. The *Eagle* came round the bend, grandly and quite quietly, a destroyer on either side of her. She looked so superb that she made me immensely proud. She dropped anchor, and then did what I had expected of her, letting off a salvo in salute to a foreign country.

Apparently my tea companions thought that war had been declared! In a single moment they had disappeared! It was a great help to me, for I collected all the éclairs that I could, and had a gorgeous feast! I could never have done it if someone else had been around. It was a glorious moment.

When I look back and think of life as it was then, watching the polo, trying to catch lizards, and all that sunshine, I remember it as being an unbelievable world. I loved seeing Europe, and it was an enormous help to me in my writing.

Robbie and I were often apart, of course, which both of us hated, but when he came back from the Mediterranean, it might be to a shore job – that was if we had any luck. It was all a matter of luck, they told me, but I thought possibly there was a lot in giving luck a shove. One learns in Fleet Street that meeting the right people at the right time makes all the difference in the world.

I was now earning far more than I had ever done before, and I needed it, for the naval pay was most revoltingly low. I really cannot think how people with nothing else lived on it.

Robbie came home on leave, and we went home to stay in the village for a holiday. Whitchurch was something of a change after going around Europe, but it always is very close to my own heart, and there I feel completely and utterly at home. It *is* to me.

It was at this time that Robbie got the job in Portsmouth, three years with an appointment to H.M.S. *Vernon*, and the two words 'shore job' thrilled me.

I should hate parting with Rose, the darling maid who had been with me all through, because she had always been so good to me. She married in my flat, and when I left for Pompey, she went to her home in Sheering near Harlow. I often visit her. She helped me say goodbye to the furniture, and it rolled away from my doors. We could not take it with us down to Pompey, so it would go into store for the time being.

All my life I have been subject to premonitions and I detest them. Suddenly life gives me a faint warning of something ahead; it is not particularly clear and with it comes a vague apprehension, a distant fear, or, far more seldom, joy! I have no control over it, I never welcome it, and it was with this apprehension, that Pip and I started for Pompey.

There had been some mistake over the trains.

I had watched the furniture depart, and had then caught the train, and now here we were, in that most dismal station at Portsmouth, and there was no Robbie to meet us. I remember sitting there with Pip, with no idea of what to do next, for I was not sure where we were going. During that time, I was alarmed by this wretched sense of apprehension, which I could not dismiss. *Go home*, said Fate. *Go back to London.*

That was when Robbie turned up.

After one or two changes, we settled in at the most charming home-from-home boarding-house on Southsea front, the Glenlyon. This was run by a little old lady, known as 'Auntie Welldon' and living with her was a very nice niece, and her brother ('Tiggy') who did the accounts. The Glenlyon was as near to home as anything you could have had, and I owe those people a lot, because I was so happy there.

It was almost entirely R.N.

But Southsea was not a help to me. I had not been feeling well
for quite a time, and it was here that I started to suffer from bad
headaches. They came unexpectedly out of the blue, and I could
not associate them with any particular thing. I found that in those
days I never went anywhere without aspirins in my handbag. I
remembered that my father had been subject to headaches at
Whitchurch. Had I inherited these? They increased rapidly. I got
to the stage when I consulted various doctors, but the headache is
an elusive thing, and there can be too many reasons for it. Most
of them blamed my work. "Do less work and enjoy yourself,"
they said.

Now Robbie never danced, he did not like it. This meant that I
gave it up, and it had meant a tremendous lot to me, for I was
good at it. He was used to what I should have thought was a far
duller form of life than I was, and when it came to living there in
Pompey, this told on me.

How I hated the place, and it had such a hideous beach, such
bad bathing, and was such an ugly town! The only things I liked
apart from the Glenlyon, were Handley's shop, and the chocolate
shop where they had a special line on Saturdays, and often it was
my favourite chocolate gingers!

We had three years there, and although I was doing well
financially, and taking interesting holidays abroad, I was
wretched. Then Robbie finished there and joined H.M.S. *Hood*,
and for the time being I went to live in the Onslow Court Hotel
in South Kensington. Dear Miss Willatt ran it, and was always
kind to me; I must say that I was very happy there.

But these headaches were tormenting me. Could it be that my
life was not the normal one, and that when one lives in a way
that is different, it does not always help? I had the doctor I had
had in Battersea, kind Dr Rowland, who was a most marvellous
man (a half-caste) and he always said that the mistake his white
father had made was bringing him here to England to make a
doctor of him. He was quite wonderful, and all Battersea would
back me in this. The last time I saw him he was very ill, and I and
his wife went together to visit him in hospital. His last remark

was, "The trouble with God is that He has no sense of humour!" I believe he was right.

The headaches worsened. I had a couple of operations which did not do the slightest bit of good, and I was considerably poorer after them than before.

Then one day, when Pip was on holiday from Cirencester Royal Agricultural College, he and I went for a little walk round Chelsea. Robbie had retired by now. He had become aware of these increasing headaches, and often I was knocked out for days at a time by them; he most nobly gave up the Navy. He got a job at the Foreign Office, nothing with a fat purse attached of course — that never seemed to happen — but I could work, and did.

On this particular day Pip and I wandered into Chelsea and admired a new enormous block of flats which had just been opened. They were called Cranmer Court. Out of curiosity we poked our noses into one of these. They had been built on a piece of Chelsea which had been the old fairground, and we fell in love with the ground floor flat that we saw. It was utterly charming, and had everything one could possibly want.

We discussed it together. What would Robbie think of it? We liked it so much, and wanted to live there so that we made a little plan. There was a very charming girl who had taken us round, and we told her we might be back that afternoon, bringing my husband with us.

She said that would be quite all right.

"Oh, I *do* hope he likes it," said Pip.

"We have got to do something about this one," I told him.

We started being what we hoped would be clever. That afternoon we took Robbie for a little walk on the excuse that it was such a nice day! We strolled languidly into Chelsea, and drew his attention to the enormous block of flats built on the old fairground. He was a little more oncoming than we had expected, for he is not usually a very enthusiastic person. Pip got the key from the same pleasant girl and we went round the ground floor flat together. I must say that Robbie walked most innocently into the trap, and he fell in love with the place. Cranmer Court at that time had the most amazing head porter (a

Beefeater amongst other things!) and we had an extremely good management. I took the flat then and there, and moved in as soon as it was decorated to my taste. This meant that I should have a home of my own again, somewhere to lay my aching head without any bother, and the flat *was* a most brilliant success.

The work increased as though by magic. I was on the *Sunday Pictorial*, with Hugh Cudlipp, I did the letters for *Home Notes*, and was beauty editor on *Woman's Own*, with Constance Holt as editor. And with all this, I would produce at least four short stories a week, and a couple of full-length novels a year, with the occasional extra book.

We were living in Cranmer Court when the war came, and at first of course everything went well. Things were so calm that first winter that we thought Hitler had realized that he had made a mistake and was now trying to get out of it. How wrong we were, of course! In my personal life, Pip's marriage had broken, and he had come back home for help. He went through the divorce, and that was that. Then the war came along and we had that long dull winter when we believed that nothing was going to happen after all, then all of a sudden it happened.

I shall never forget that late spring when the war first burst on us in full vigour. The Foreign Office job was moved out of London, and we went with it, then we came back again. The raids became unbelievably worse, and I moved into another flat. I had not been in it a week before a land mine came down on Cranmer Court. I never even heard it, for I was knocked out, and so was Robbie, lying in our passage-way, to come to with the walls all broken around us, and fire engines playing on the skeleton of the flats that had been.

That is the sort of thing that one asks to forget.

There seemed to be little point in staying on here, and on the advice of my doctor I went down to Letchworth. His wife and children were staying in a hotel there, and he thought it would be very suitable, which it was.

That was a filthy war.

At this time I was doing a lot of plays for the B.B.C., Val Gielgud was a very easy man to work for, but all the time the headaches were shocking, and I don't think the conditions under which we were living were a tremendous help. I made up my mind that the moment we were through with wartime living, I should have to get something done, for the pain was a bit too much.

We lived the life of all people in wars. I was down at Brighton during the last winter, going to London two days a week to work, always on the alert for the crash that told me that another bomb had come down. It was all very difficult. During this time Pip re-married, far more suitably, and when the war ended they were expecting their first baby.

I came back to London just before peace day.

It was such a changed London. I still had a flat in Cranmer Court (the other side of it); one side was still completely shattered, you could see right through it. I had planned a wild celebration on peace day, but that celebration never came off. I was almost semi-conscious with my head. It was a miracle, though, that we were through with the war. Now what? We sang *God Who made her mighty, make her mightier yet*, with patriotic fervour, but I must say I did not feel "mightier yet". When the conquering armies marched through London, perhaps we were great for the last time?

9

MY CAREER

It was one afternoon in summer, a great moment in my life, when Charles Eade, editor of the *Sunday Dispatch*, sent for me. I had by then quite forgotten a piece I had done quickly for him at the start of the war; he had been pleased with my promptitude (I am an extremely punctual person) delivering it a quarter of an hour early, and he had said that he would not forget me. I thought that he had forgotten me, when he rang me up, and said he had a proposition to make to me.

I had thought by this time that he had other writers, for an entire war lay between then and now. Robbie took me along to the offices in the car, wondering, as I did, what all this was about. I went into the hall of Northcliffe House, knowing that something funny was going on, because the head porter came forward so urbanely to receive me and took me up in the special visitors' lift, not the usual one.

I said that this was a bit odd, but he said oh no, it was orders, and hadn't it been a nice day? and a lot more of that sort of thing.

There was Charles in his office, a very small man, and at first he was most evasive, as these men always are. We had some tea, and talked about everything in the world, except why I had come here, and what was going on. Then he came down to it.

He was looking for a very strong serial, to put his sales up, and he wanted something on Emma Hamilton. Now I had never done a historical book in my life, and I said that seeing that I had had a very sparse education I did not think I was the right person to do this. He said that he knew I was, I wish I knew how he knew!

He wanted twenty instalments for a start (in the end it actually ran into thirty-five of them) and I had to leave what are called 'open doors' so that more could be added when needed. I was, of course, wildly interested, but never thought that I could do it. Charles had a blind faith in me, he was convinced that he had got a winner, and how right he was!

I was to do two instalments for him to see and then we would go further into the matter. Rather limply I returned to Robbie in the car, and when I told him about it, he came to the conclusion that Charles has gone mad! (So like a husband!)

Then he asked, "What is he paying you for this?" and when he heard, he could not believe it. "He'll get the sack," he said, as the car turned into Fleet Street.

The street of adventure … I'll say! I told myself.

I wrote the serial, and to my dismay Charles sat on it for quite a time. It would not come out under my own name, and as I could not think of a *nom de plume*, I foolishly left this to Charles. Later I went to see him, and he told me with triumph that the serial was coming out under the name of Lozania Prole.

I very nearly fainted with shock! When I asked how he had got hold of this name, he told me, *Lozanía* was Spanish for a blossom (Bloom); he had been in Spain recently where he had thought this out. *Prole* was Spanish for a seed. His name was C. Eade, and there you were. He felt that as he had given me the idea for the contribution, he ought to be in it. I thought that the name was quite dreadful, but it was my fault for giving him a free hand with it, and there was not a word I could say save "Thank you, very much." Privately I was not amused.

It was *Our Dearest Emma* that started me on the historical path, possibly inherited from my father's historical interests, only I had been unaware of it.

When the serial began, the sales went up enormously, and I offered the novel to my publishers, Hutchinson. I was horrified when they refused it. I wrote to dear Mrs Webb (the head of their book department), and I am sure that it was the time at which the book was offered to her that had influenced her. Hale eventually published it and it sold on a million copies. Hutchinson had had a wretched court case, and poor Mrs Webb had had to go to court for the firm and take most of the blame.

She was suffering badly from shock, and I do indeed realize how she felt, but I could have wept that I had not done the work for the firm which was so closely connected with me. I felt that I owed them this, because they had been the people who had started me on my novels.

Robert Hale, whom I had known when he was with Hutchinson in the early days, chased me all round London to get it, and he got it. He could never have regretted that.

I continued working for Charles, and enjoyed every moment of it. I did the Florence Nightingale serial, Ruth Ellis, the Crippen case, and a whole heap of them.

In his office he had hanging behind him on the wall big photographs of those people who had put his sales up above all others. I always envied them. Churchill was there, and Eisenhower, Kathleen Winsor, and two others. One day when I went in, *my own photograph was with them*. I had got there, and I could not believe it.

Walter Hutchinson had now left St Paul's Churchyard and he had enormous offices of a very handsome kind. We had always got on well together, and once he had paid me the greatest compliment that I have ever had, saying, to my face "You are the most blithering little idiot I have ever met, but you can do some damned good work, and I like you."

Now that *is* an honour, and I said so.

Working for the *Sunday Dispatch* was a real joy. It was my great comfort with those shocking headaches, as though writing were the guardian angel behind me, helping me through all the time. It has always given me a certain courage of its own, and with it, one can enter a sort of ghost world which has a tale to tell, a world inhabited by people who will never breathe, but who come to life on the printed page.

I love it.

I wish that Fleet Street had not changed so much. Gone are the days when there were dozens of papers and magazines wanting work, and editors to meet and help authors. There used to be hordes of them, but the world has changed enormously. Perhaps the first red light of the changing world came to me when we were living at Frinton, and the tweenie married a major and brought him in to tea with her. Denham, seeing red, said, "My God! Now shall I have to call him 'sir'? It's the end."

It probably *was* the end in all senses of the word.

The home has suffered worst of all. My father always predicted that this would happen, and how he hated it! Many things needed changing, of course, and some of them were to the good, but they changed too much and too fast. I do not think that equality is possible in a world where we are basically unequal. Today too many of us have to cut out the work which could help others, because we have menial duties to do, and then get too tired. Everything, even faith itself, has been altered.

Before the Second World War came I went out to review the Passion Play at Oberammergau for a magazine. Adolf Hitler had been there the week before I went. He was just coming into power, tremendously admired by the people, and of immense promise. What a shame it was that it all went the wrong way, for he could have been such a help to a difficult world instead of the maniac that he became. Whatever one may say, Oberammergau is the only place that I have visited where the people were completely Christian. They helped one.

It is the only time in my life that I have ever lived for a few hours with a people who were practising the Christianity of the Bible. Nothing was too much for them to do for one.

I was worried to death that I would come on with one of my violent headaches and would arrive a trifle late at the play, because I had heard that, if this happened, they would not let you in. What should I do then? The sweet woman who ran the solicitor's house where I was staying told me not to be afraid. Of course they would let me in. I said that people doubted you when pleading a bad headache, because so many used this as an excuse when nothing at all was the matter with them. She stared at me in amazement, and said, "But if you say it, of course it is true."

That is their angle, and the strange thing is that their own virtue makes you like them! *They* could only speak the truth, and you knew it.

I spent two nights there (one is not allowed to stay longer) and

Pip and I found ourselves behaving to each other most strangely after it. We were quite polite on all occasions telling none of those ordinary little lies that always slip into everyday life, and it was extremely odd.

The play itself did not affect me as emotionally as I had anticipated it would. Of course it is always difficult to follow anything in another language, even though they do supply you with the most complete translation. I arrived a little late and was considerably upset to find Pip sitting there in the full national dress, which he had got up early to go out and buy for himself. While the play is actually on, all the shops are shut and no business is done.

One of the most thrilling moments came very early in the morning (it would have been about half past seven) when the little donkey on which Christ would ride, was led through the town on his way to the dressing-rooms.

The play was performed by people who believe absolutely. I was enormously impressed by the huge tableaux when very young children stood like statues, and this is *not* easy. It had extreme beauty when Christ was on the cross, but somehow one got the impression that He never rose again. He walked on from the side on ground level, of course, and this was where it failed.

I was very glad to have seen it, though the visit gave me a dreadful uneasiness about Herr Hitler. What was the future going to be?

But it was now that the headaches began to grow even worse. I awoke in agony, and this pain could be unbearable. I got sick of Harley Street, and I had to fight every inch of the way with this abiding pain. I was sick of going to strange and expensive consultants, and getting nothing in the way of success. Half of them did not even believe what I said, but blamed the headaches on overwork. But in the end the way was shown to me. It came in a strange manner, and although I have told this before, I tell it again, if only to prove that although we think we live this life of ours alone, this is not true.

I heard of a doctor who did a very special operation for this sort of headache, which meant the severing of a nerve. A friend of some friends of ours had had it done, and suddenly, in desperation, I went to this man. I know that I took my courage in my own hands and, when visiting him, only Robbie and myself knew that I was doing it.

I am a curious person for taking likes and dislikes, and can be very fond of the most odd people, and hate awfully nice ones for no known reason. The man was much older than I had anticipated he would be, rather gruff, and I did not like him, but he could and would do it. Then and there we arranged for a bed in hospital, and an anaesthetist. I felt that if I did not do it straight away, I should never get it done.

I drove home, not entirely pleased, because I did not like the man, and that night I got a telephone message from some friends living in Brighton. They were having the most lovely weather down there, they said, why not come down on Sunday and have lunch with them and make the most of it? Also they were the people whose friend had had this operation, it would be nice if we met. I said that I should love to go. It would take my mind off things.

Just as we were finishing talking, the friend said, "Oh, by the way, be careful when talking to our friend, for I don't think I told you, but that op. made her blind. It can do that."

I nearly fainted. So this was behind the apprehension which had suddenly overwhelmed me! Next morning I cancelled all the arrangements.

But the pain went on slowly killing me, and in the end I met the surgeon who really did help me. At first we got on badly, but he was very patient, asking all sorts of questions and taking far more trouble than anybody else. Then he operated on the trigeminal nerve.

On the day itself, I thought that everything was going all wrong, for it was an afternoon operation, which I always hate (too much waiting about). The stretcher party were dears and so kind … When I came round it was difficult to speak, but no pain at all, which they had promised me. But doctors are *not* always truthful.

It entailed a lot of plastic surgery later, but here I was fortunate, for one of the Galer grand-daughters had married a brilliant plastic surgeon, a German, and the Germans do this work so much better than our own men. He rebuilt my face, bless him!

I can never speak highly enough of what that man did for me, the goodness of his nurses, and the kindness that I received. For a time an eye was damaged, and I had to wear a shade, but the headaches had gone for ever. There are people in this world to whom one owes everything, and what I feel for that surgeon is a tremendous debt of gratitude.

On the whole, life is unfair in the way it works out. It is a game played without an umpire! I have come to the conclusion that this is no fun, and also that there is no way of avoiding the darts of outrageous fortune. If I were asked to do it, I don't think that I *could* live my life again.

It began with those early childhood difficulties of a flirtatious father (in a profession which does not encourage this sort of thing, only he never seemed to know that). My parents' separation, which, at the time, very nearly broke my heart. It must be a very tough heart to stand up to what it has stood up to!

It went on with living through years when Mother was dying from, perhaps the most cruel disease of them all, when it was difficult to get enough to eat. I had two years' marriage with that poor young man who had never had a chance, and I, who could have helped him, came into his life when it was already too late to save him.

One cannot foresee the future, of course, for Fate has an eerie method of turning round on one and hitting when and where one least expects to receive the blow. There never was such a villain as Fate, if you ask me.

But in spite of the bitter disappointments, and the way life seems never to have given me a gift without, as an old friend one said, "wrapping it in a shroud", the pen has given me immense happiness. It began at two years old, when I scribbled on the soles of my shoes, signs which I said were "tories". Without this solace and this comfort to me, my heart would have broken years ago. It was the pen that pulled me through. Without it I could not have lived, and that is the truth.